HOMEMADE
PRESENTS

HOMEMADE PRESENTS

Inspiring Gift Ideas to Share

Marlies Busch

h.f.ullmann

Contents

Given with Love

German Romantic poet Novalis was right when he wrote that what we harvest in summer becomes the gifts of winter. So we cook and bake, we preserve fruit and vegetables in oils or alcohol, and they make wonderful gifts. Beautifully wrapped and presented with love, these small gifts will bring great pleasure and joy, whatever the season.

Foreword

Giving gifts is one of the bases of our civilization; it's a practice that strengthens social bonds, brings joy to others, and demonstrates our love and affection. Nothing could be nicer than a present chosen, and given, with care. It may not seem to make strict financial sense to give something away without expecting something in return, but gift-giving is an essential part of our society. Those who see one present as a response to another have misunderstood the principle entirely, and risk the same fate that befell the indigenous tribes of Canada, who, at the "potlatch" (a traditional gift-giving meeting), would strive to outdo each other in their generosity until they had nothing left to give. In order to avoid any such damaging and drastic outcomes, I have come up with a selection of small but thoughtful presents for you to make and share. They are not expensive in terms of cost, but they do require a little time, and nowadays, that is the most precious gift we have.

The things we harvest in summer
Will be gifts for us in winter.
Novalis

Gifts from the Kitchen

These edible treats will delight all your friends. Gifts from the kitchen are both much appreciated by the recipient and quick to make, even if you don't have a garden or backyard of your own and have to buy the ingredients. Jams, small cakes, or even little bottles of homemade flavored vinegar are always welcome at dinner parties as small tokens of thanks. In terms of the effort invested, they are the most precious of gifts. All that time spent in the kitchen baking cakes, making preserves, and bottling delicious fruits really shows in the finished product.

I have come up with a wide variety of ideas for culinary gifts that look as good as they taste, so you're bound to find something for every occasion. With their pretty wrapping and original labels, these presents will steal the show from any store-bought present.

Rhubarb Jam

Bring out the zing in rhubarb with this recipe. It is a great way to preserve its flavor and is like capturing early summer in a jar. Delicious in desserts and cakes, and a natural partner for bread, this jam makes a welcome gift.

▦ Trim and wash the rhubarb. Discard the poisonous leaves, but keep the trimmings. You can use them to make delicious syrup (see page 20).

▦ Cut the stems into small pieces, wash, and place in a pan with the sugar, vanilla sugar or the scraped-out seeds of the vanilla bean, and salt. Stir well and let the mixture stand for about 1 hour to allow the rhubarb juice to be drawn out.

▦ Bring to a boil, stirring continuously, and cook at low simmer until the rhubarb breaks down and loses its shape. Transfer the warm mixture to sterilized jars, seal, and turn upside down on a dish towel for five minutes before cooling. The jam will keep for 3–4 months in a cool place.

Gooseberry Jam

INGREDIENTS

2¼ lb/1 kg
gooseberries
Generous ¾ cup/
200 ml apple juice
1–2 tbsp lemon juice,
to taste
2¼ cups/500 g jam
sugar

The apple juice softens the acidity of the gooseberries in this recipe and adds an interesting note to the jam. Green gooseberries are a little more sour than red ones; if you have a sweet tooth, you might want to leave out the lemon juice. Gooseberry jam makes a popular present.

▓ Top, tail, and wash the gooseberries and place in a pan with the apple juice, lemon juice, and sugar.

▓ Bring to a boil, stirring continuously, and cook at a rolling boil for 3–4 minutes.

▓ To test for a set, put a saucer in the freezer to chill. Spoon a little of the jam onto the chilled saucer, then push a finger across the jam. If it wrinkles and is starting to set then it's ready, if not cook for 5 minutes longer and test again.

▓ Transfer the jam to sterilized jars, seal, and turn upside down on a dish towel for five minutes before cooling. The jam will keep in the refrigerator for a good 3–4 months.

Blackberry and Apple Jam

INGREDIENTS

Generous 1 lb/500 g
apples
1 bunch thyme
3½ tbsp/50 ml water
or apple juice
Generous 1 lb/500 g
blackberries
2¼ cups/500 g jam
sugar

The combination of blackberries and apples with thyme makes this jam particularly interesting. The first rule of making gifts is to give others only things you would be happy to receive yourself, and this certainly fits the bill.

▓ Peel, core, and dice the apples before cooking them with the thyme and the water or apple juice to form a puree.

▓ Remove the sprigs of thyme and mix the puree with the crushed blackberries and the sugar. Let steep for a few hours.

▓ Bring the mixture to a rolling boil and then boil for 4–5 minutes, before testing for a set (see page 13). Transfer the jam to sterilized jars, seal, and turn upside down on a dish towel for five minutes before cooling. The jam will keep for 3–4 months in a cool place.

Pear and Sichuan Pepper Jam

INGREDIENTS

2¼ lb/1 kg pears (e.g. Williams or Bartlett)
1 tbsp lemon juice
1 tbsp orange juice
Grated zest of
1 unwaxed lemon
Grated zest of
1 unwaxed orange
3 oz/80 g fresh ginger
1 tbsp Sichuan pepper
Scant 3¼ cups/700 g jam sugar
1⅓ cups/7 oz/200 g shelled almonds

This pepper-spiked pear jam complements game or cheese really well, but you can also enjoy it with pancakes.

▦ Quarter, core, and dice the pears before mixing with the lemon juice, orange juice, and zest. Peel the ginger, cut into thin slices, and scatter over the fruit, along with the pepper and sugar. Let steep for at least 1 hour.

▦ Bring to a boil over high heat and cook for 5–10 minutes, stirring continuously until the consistency starts to thicken. Add the almonds.

▦ Transfer to hot sterilized jars, seal, and turn upside down on a dish towel for five minutes before cooling.

VARIATION

A small amount of star anise will give this pear jam extra zing.

Spiced Bottled Cherries

Add a decorated scroll with the secret recipe for this delicious preserve to make a charming present.

INGREDIENTS

2¼ lb/1 kg sweet cherries
7 tbsp/100 ml red wine vinegar
Generous ¾ cup/200 ml red wine
3 tbsp pink peppercorns
1½ cups/300 g sugar
1 stick of cinnamon
3 cloves

Plump cherries in a preserving jar look beautiful and taste delicious. They make the perfect gift to take to dinner parties.

▥ Wash and pit the cherries and place in a clean bowl. Mix in all the other ingredients, place a weighted plate on top, and let steep overnight.

▥ The following day, strain the cherries, reserving the juice. Reduce the juice to about half the volume in a pan, add the cherries from the strainer, and bring everything back to a boil.

▥ Transfer the peppered cherries to sterilized jars that are still hot and seal well; they will keep for 6–8 weeks. The cherries make a wonderful accompaniment to game, beef, and veal steaks.

Fruity Rumtopf

VARIATION

Add a stick of
cinnamon and a little
star anise for a more
complex flavor. The
fruit will keep for up
to 4 months.

INGREDIENTS

Approx. 7 oz/200 g
each strawberries,
raspberries, blue-
berries, blackberries,
sour cherries,
peaches, apricots,
and plums (3 lb/
1.4 kg in total)
Scant 3¼ cups/
700 g sugar
3–4 cups/700 ml–
1 liter rum

Rumtopf means "rum pot" and is a traditional German and Danish dessert, usually not eaten until the first day of Advent (although some people just cannot wait that long!). It makes perfect use of summer fruits and is a wonderful and very personal Christmas present.

■ Pick the summer fruits when they are ripe and layer them in a sterilized jar or bottle; preserve them using two parts fruit to one part sugar and one part rum.

■ The rum should always completely cover the fruit; to make sure the fruit remains immersed, you may need to use a small plate to weigh it down.

Rhubarb Syrup

9 oz/250 g rhubarb
trimmings (not the
leaves)
4½ cups/1 kg sugar
2 tsp/10 g citric acid

This syrup is absolutely delicious with a dash of sparkling wine but is also fine for enjoying every day when diluted with water. For this recipe, you could use the trimmings left over from making rhubarb jam (see page 12). NB Do not use/eat the leaves.

▧ Wash the rhubarb thoroughly before preparing. Bring the trimmings to a boil in 1 quart/1 liter water with the sugar and the citric acid and reduce to form a syrup.

▧ Let the syrup cool, then pass through a strainer. Return to a boil and transfer the still-hot syrup to sterilized bottles and seal tightly. Store in as cool a place as possible. Properly sealed, the syrup will keep for 1–2 months.

TIP

Diluted with water,
the syrup makes a
wonderfully refresh-
ing cordial for hot
summer days.

Black Currant Syrup

4½ lb/2 kg black
currants
Juice of 1 lemon
4½ cups/1 kg sugar

Sun-ripened black currants combined with sugar make this syrup absolutely delicious. It can be enjoyed for many months after the black currant bush has been stripped bare.

▧ Wash the berries and briefly bring to a boil in ⅔ cup/150 ml water until they form a puree, then pass through a cheesecloth or muslin cloth.

▧ Bring the juice to a boil with the lemon juice and the sugar, cook at a rolling boil for 2–3 minutes. Transfer the still-hot syrup to sterilized bottles and seal tightly.

▧ Let cool completely, and store in a cool, dry place, where the syrup will keep for 3–4 months.

VARIATION

A stick of cinnamon
or a vanilla bean will
add an extra flavor
dimension to the
syrup.

Onion Chutney

INGREDIENTS

Generous 1 lb/500 g
onions
1 tbsp oil
1 tbsp sugar
7 tbsp/100 ml red
wine vinegar
1 bay leaf
1 clove
2 tbsp honey
1 tbsp butter
1 sprig parsley
Salt and pepper
Cayenne pepper
1 tbsp lingonberries

This recipe for onion chutney is a spicy variation on the theme and is given a sophisticated edge by the addition of the lingonberries. It goes well with any grilled dishes, especially meat and game.

▪ Peel the onions, cut into thin rings, and fry in the oil and sugar over low heat until translucent. Deglaze the pan with the red wine vinegar, add the bay leaf and clove, then simmer the mixture over low heat for about 45 minutes. You might need to add a little more water.

▪ Add the honey, butter, and chopped parsley, and season with salt, pepper, and cayenne pepper. Pick out any bad lingonberries and stir in the rest. Remove the bay leaf and clove, and transfer the chutney to sterilized screw-top preserving jars while it is still hot. The chutney will keep for 3–4 weeks.

VARIATION

A sprig of fresh oregano works well in this recipe, either in the chutney or as decoration.

Onions in Red Wine

Ingredients

3¼ lb/1.5 kg onions
2 quarts/2 liters
salted water
1 tbsp olive oil
Salt
Scant ¾ cup/150 g
confectioners' (icing)
sugar
½ cup/125 ml red
wine
2 bay leaves
½ cup/125 ml red
wine vinegar
Pepper

These onions make a perfect dinner party gift, not to mention a delicious accompaniment to grilled food and game dishes.

▣ Peel the onions and cut into rings. Blanch for a few minutes in salted water, then drain, reserving the liquid.

▣ Fry the drained onions in olive oil until translucent, then season with salt and dredge with the sugar. Deglaze the pan with the red wine, add the bay leaves, and bring the mixture to a boil.

▣ Add 1 cup/250 ml of the onion liquid along with the vinegar, and bring back to a boil, seasoning with salt and pepper.

▣ Place a lid on the pan and let steep overnight. The following day, bring back to a boil and transfer the onions to sterilized jars while still hot. Top off with the spicy liquid and seal. The onions will keep for 4–6 weeks.

Variation

You can also use small shallots for this dish, halved or whole.

Tomato Chutney

INGREDIENTS

3¼ lb/1.5 kg
tomatoes
9 cups/2 kg jam
sugar
Juice of 2 limes

This recipe is an excellent way of using up a glut of tomatoes from your garden or backyard and also makes a very attractive Christmas present.

■ Wash the tomatoes and chop into large pieces, trimming off the green part near the stalk. Mix the tomato chunks with the sugar in a pan, bring to a boil, and simmer for about 20 minutes until the mixture has reached the consistency of a jam.

■ Add lime juice to taste and transfer the chutney to sterilized jars while still hot. Seal the jars and let stand upside down for 5 minutes. The chutney will keep in the refrigerator for about 2–3 months and tastes just as good on bread as it does with game dishes or cheese.

GIFT INSPIRATION

I put my homemade chutney in a pretty screw-top or Mason jar when presenting it as a gift.

Apple and
Tomato Jam

INGREDIENTS

2¼ lb/1 kg ripe
tomatoes
2¼ lb/1 kg apples
4½ cups/1 kg
jam sugar
2 tbsp lemon juice
1 tsp ground mace
5 sprigs thyme
2 cloves

Beautiful apples and tomatoes are still in season in the fall and make a delicious combination.

◼ Peel the tomatoes and cut into quarters, removing the green part near the stalk. Peel, core, and dice the apples. Combine with the sugar, lemon juice, mace, thyme, and cloves. Add the tomatoes and bring briefly to a boil and heat through.

◼ Remove the apples and tomatoes, using a slotted spoon, and set aside. Bring the liquid back to a boil until it begins to thicken.

◼ Return the apples and tomatoes to the pan and transfer the jam to sterilized jars, sealing them well. Let stand upside down for a few minutes. This jam will keep for 3–4 months if well chilled.

GIFT
INSPIRATION

Turn simple jam jars into lovely gifts for friends by tying pretty tissue paper around the lid as decoration.

Potted Liverwurst

Liverwurst, or liver sausage, is quick and easy to make and has a very sophisticated flavor. It is not expensive and homemade liverwurst is always impressive.

■ Dice the calf's liver; chop two thirds of it coarsely and blitz it with a handheld blender to a puree, then chop the remainder of the liver finely.

■ Peel and dice the shallots. Fry them in a small amount of butter with the chopped and pureed liver, adding a little thyme and then seasoning the mixture with salt and pepper.

■ Melt the butter carefully in a bowl placed over a simmering pan of water (it shouldn't go brown), and add the cognac and the cream before stirring this mixture into the fried liver.

■ Transfer to a sterilized jar or a small terrine and decorate with a sprig of thyme. It is particularly delicious when served with lingonberry jam and black bread. Liverwurst will keep for about 3–4 days in the refrigerator.

VARIATION

Add rosemary or red peppercorns for extra flavor.

INGREDIENTS

Generous 1 lb/500 g
calf's liver
2 shallots
1 cup + 2 tbsp/250 g
butter, plus butter for
frying
Approx. 2 tbsp
stripped thyme
Salt and pepper
1 tbsp cognac
1 tbsp light (single)
cream
1 sprig thyme

Country Style Lard Spread with Cracklings

VARIATION

Pink peppercorns give the spread a bit of an extra kick. A cappuccino mug makes a stylish and unusual container for your edible gift.

INGREDIENTS

2¼ lb/1 kg pork belly (pork fat/leaf lard)

It is hard to beat this delicious homemade lard spread or drippings, known as pork schmalz in Germany, as a special treat when spread on rye bread fresh from the oven and sprinkled with a pinch of salt. Pork drippings are made from fatty pork belly (also known as belly fat, kidney fat, or leaf lard) and should be as fresh as possible.

▧ Cut the fat into small pieces or put it through the coarse disk of a meat grinder.

▧ Melt by heating carefully in a heavy cast-iron skillet (do not use a nonstick pan); if the cracklings (meat) inside burn, it will spoil the quality of the drippings. Good pork lard, which has only a faint aroma of its own, should be white and easy to spread.

▧ Strain through a cheesecloth or muslin cloth, removing the bits of meat first and then replacing them if desired.

▧ Transfer to sterilized jars. A slight skin will form on the surface once the lard has cooled. It will keep for about 3 months in the refrigerator.

Tasty Mini Quiches

VARIATION

Add some fresh asparagus and shredded Parmesan to the quiches in the spring months; chervil will add a piquant note.

INGREDIENTS

9 oz/250 g all-purpose (plain) flour
8½ tbsp/125 g cold butter
6 eggs
1¾ oz/50 g dried tomatoes
2 scallions (spring onions)
1 zucchini (courgette)
1 clove of garlic
3½ oz/100 g Gruyère, shredded
1⅔ cups/400 ml light (single) cream
Salt and pepper
Chives and sour cream, to garnish

These cute quiches look attractive and taste delicious. They are the perfect size for presents and you could even include a pretty label with the handwritten recipe.

■ Mix the flour with a pinch of salt and make a well in the middle. Cut the butter into small pieces and place in the well with one egg. Work the dough briskly with your hands. Wrap the dough in foil and chill in the refrigerator for about 1 hour.

■ Soften the dried tomatoes briefly in lukewarm water, then chop finely. Clean and trim the scallions and cut into rings. Wash and shred the zucchini, peel and finely chop the garlic, then mix all the vegetables together.

■ Whisk the remaining 5 eggs, mixing in the shredded cheese and the cream. Season with salt and pepper.

■ Preheat the oven to 360°F/180°C. Roll out the dough, and use it to line the greased mini-tart pans. Bake blind in the preheated oven for 5 minutes. Put a small amount of the vegetables in each tart and top with the egg and cream mixture. Bake for around 20–25 minutes. Garnish with chives and a little sour cream; the quiches will taste good served either warm or cold.

Small Mushroom Pies

These take no time to make and taste absolutely delicious. If you want to ensure they are homemade from start to finish, harvest the mushrooms yourself (taking care that you harvest only edible mushrooms), or you can of course use store-bought products. Nicely wrapped, these pies make a lovely present.

▨ Let the puff pastry thaw. Clean the mushrooms with a dry brush but don't wash. Peel the shallot and dice, along with the mushrooms and bacon.

▨ Heat a little oil in a skillet and fry the shallot until translucent, then add the bacon and mushrooms and fry off. Season with salt and pepper, and let cool.

▨ Wash the herbs and chop finely. Whisk the crème fraîche with the eggs, fold in the herbs, and season the mixture to taste.

▨ Roll out the puff pastry and use a cutter or a jar as a template to cut out 10–12 circles with a diameter of 5–6 inches/12–15 cm. Use the remaining scraps of dough to make strips to place over the tops of the pies.

▨ Preheat the oven to 390°F/200°C. Grease the cups of a muffin pan and line with the circles of dough. Place a little of the mushroom mixture in each pie and pour over the egg mixture. Top the pies with pastry strips. Bake for about 30 minutes until golden and serve hot or cold.

TIP

Use the same recipe to make a large pie with a diameter of 14 inches/35 cm. You will need to extend the baking time for about 15 minutes.

INGREDIENTS

1 lb/450 g frozen puff pastry (store-bought)
14 oz/400 g mushrooms (depending on season—girolles, field mushrooms, ceps, oyster mushrooms)
1 shallot
2½ oz/75 g bacon
Olive oil
Salt and pepper
1 bunch chives
1 bunch parsley
10 tbsp/150 g crème fraîche or sour cream
4 eggs
Butter for greasing

Peppermint Oil

INGREDIENTS

1 oz/25 g fresh
mint leaves
Iced water
1 cup/250 ml
canola (rapeseed) oil

Herbal oils are delicious and a great treat to receive. If you arrive as a guest with a bottle of peppermint oil in your hand, you will receive a warm welcome.

◼ Wash the mint leaves and pat them dry carefully. Have a bowl of iced water to hand.

◼ Boil some water in a pan and briefly blanch the mint leaves; remove and refresh in the iced water. Remove the leaves, squeeze them out carefully, and dry between two sheets of paper towel.

◼ Whizz the leaves in a blender to form a puree, gradually adding the oil in batches. Strain through a cheesecloth or muslin cloth, and transfer the oil to a sterilized bottle.

◼ The oil will keep in the refrigerator for 5–6 months, but should be brought to room temperature before use in order to allow its full aroma to develop.

Thyme Chili Oil

INGREDIENTS

6 sprigs dried thyme
2 fresh chilis
10 black peppercorns
8 allspice seeds
1 bay leaf
1 clove
¼ tsp fennel seeds
2 cups/500 ml
cold-pressed olive oil

The slight kick of the chili blends beautifully with the thyme, turning this oil into a fragrant and piquant gift.

■ Place the sprigs of thyme in a sterilized bottle with a wide neck. Cut the chilis into strips and crush the remaining spices gently with a mortar and pestle before adding them to the bottle.

■ Pour in the oil, seal the bottle tightly, and let steep in a dark place at room temperature for 2 weeks.

■ The oil has a very intense flavor and can be diluted with the same quantity of oil again. It is a real culinary treat when used for salad dressings, as well as for stir-fry or flash-fry recipes. Thyme oil will keep for about 2 months.

GIFT INSPIRATION

Use strips of raffia to tie a few sprigs of thyme to the bottle as an attractive decoration.

Walnut Oil

INGREDIENTS

1⅓ cups/160 g
shelled walnuts
1 cup/250 ml canola
(rapeseed) oil

Walnut oil is always in great demand and its nutty flavor adds a particularly subtle dimension to salads. It is easy to make and a luxurious treat to receive. Do bear in mind, however, that it is not a cooking oil and should never be heated.

■ Lightly dry-fry the walnuts in a skillet, while warming the canola oil in an ovenproof dish in the oven. Place the walnuts in a mixer or blender, add a little warm oil, and process to form a puree. Gradually add the remaining oil.

■ Let steep for 1 day at room temperature, then strain through cheesecloth or muslin cloth, and transfer to sterilized bottles. The oil will keep in the refrigerator for up to 5 months, but should be used at room temperature to allow its full aroma to develop.

TIP

If you prefer to use olive oil, it also complements the delicate flavor of the walnuts.

Garden Vegetables in Oil

INGREDIENTS

1 zucchini
(courgette)
2 red bell peppers
1 eggplant
(aubergine)
4 shallots
1 clove of garlic
Oil for frying
Salt and pepper
5½ oz/150 g cherry
tomatoes
1 sprig basil and/or
rosemary
2 cups/500 ml
olive oil

Preserving garden vegetables in oil is a very effective way of storing them; they retain their flavor for quite some time. Add a pretty label and you have an individual gift that will be perfect to take to a winter party or a summer barbecue.

▦ Wash and cut all the vegetables into strips, apart from the cherry tomatoes.

▦ Cut the shallots into quarters, peel the garlic, and fry with the other vegetables in a splash of olive oil, seasoning with salt and pepper, to taste.

▦ Layer the vegetables in sterilized jars, adding the halved tomatoes and the basil (and/or rosemary), and topping off with the oil. The vegetables will keep in a cool place for 2–3 weeks.

Basil Pesto

INGREDIENTS

3 tbsp slivered
almonds
2 cloves garlic
3 oz/80 g basil
Generous ¾ cup/
200 ml olive oil
1 oz/30 g Parmesan
1 oz/30 g feta cheese
Salt

If time, willpower, and muscle permit, you can make a good pesto by hand using a mortar and pestle. If not, basil and almond pesto made with a mixer or blender is just as lovely to give and receive.

■ Brown the slivered almonds in a dry pan, then peel the cloves of garlic and cut into quarters. Grind the almonds, garlic, and basil in the mortar.

■ Gradually add the olive oil, the chopped Parmesan, and then the feta. To finish, season the pesto with salt and transfer to a sterilized jar. A blender will make the mixture finer and more consistent. The pesto will keep in the refrigerator for 1–2 weeks.

VARIATION

You can make a sophisticated version using macadamia nuts instead of almonds and can also use the more traditional pine nuts.

Parsley Pesto

INGREDIENTS

1 cup/100 g slivered
almonds
2 cloves garlic
1 bunch parsley
7 sage leaves
7 basil leaves
1 can (14 oz/400g)
chickpeas
Generous ¾ cup/
200 ml olive oil
3½ oz/100 g
Parmesan
Salt

Everybody loves a tasty pesto and this recipe with parsley and chickpeas delivers a particularly delicate flavor.

■ Brown the slivered almonds and crush with a **mortar** and pestle, along with the peeled and quartered garlic cloves.

■ Add the herbs and the drained chickpeas to the mixture, and work to a smooth paste before adding the oil gradually in batches.

■ Add the grated Parmesan and season with salt. Transfer to a sterilized jar. This pesto tastes fantastic with pasta and will keep for 3–4 weeks in the refrigerator.

Rosemary and Garlic Vinegar

INGREDIENTS

10 sprigs rosemary
4 cloves garlic
1 cup/250 ml light
balsamic vinegar
2½ tsp/10 g pink
peppercorns

With a pretty sprig of rosemary placed inside, these bottles of vinegar are so visually attractive that you don't really need any extra decorative touches.

■ Wash the sprigs of rosemary and pat dry; peel and halve the cloves of garlic and layer in a sterilized jar.

■ Heat the balsamic vinegar with the peppercorns, simmer briefly, and then pour over the herbs. Let cool, seal tightly, and let steep in a cool, dry place until it is the desired strength.

■ Once the vinegar has reached the required intensity, strain through a cheesecloth or muslin cloth and transfer to steril-ized bottles. Stored in a cool, dry place, the vinegar will keep for 1–2 months.

GIFT INSPIRATION

A sprig of rosemary gives the vinegar added visual appeal when displayed in a beautiful gift bottle, like those shown in the picture.

Basil and Chive Vinegar

INGREDIENTS

1 unwaxed lemon
7–8 fresh basil leaves
1 bunch fresh chives
2 cups/500 ml white
wine vinegar

■ Use a zester to peel paper-thin strips from the washed lemon. Wash the herbs, pat dry, chop coarsely, and place in a clean container with the lemon zest.

■ Heat the vinegar until hot but not boiling and then pour over the herbs. Once the mixture has cooled completely, strain the vinegar, transfer to sterilized bottles, and store in a cool, dry place, where it will keep for 1–2 months.

GIFT INSPIRATION

Present the vinegar in an attractive container, such as a small wooden box, with a few sprigs of fresh Greek basil.

Pomegranate and Vanilla Vinegar

INGREDIENTS

1 cup/150 g
pomegranate seeds
5 drops vanilla
extract
2 cups/500 ml white
wine vinegar

It's worth taking the trouble to remove every seed for this amazingly tasty pomegranate vinegar. Its exotic ingredients will make it a culinary gift to remember.

■ Cut open the pomegranate and extract the seeds. Drizzle the vanilla extract over the seeds and arrange them in layers in a sterilized glass jar.

■ Heat the vinegar until hot but not boiling and pour over the seeds, let cool, and seal tightly in a sterilized bottle. Stored in a cool, dry place, this vinegar will keep for a good 2–3 months.

TIP

You can also enjoy eating the preserved pomegranate seeds.

Rose Hip Vinegar

INGREDIENTS

2 cups/generous
1 lb/500 g fresh
rose hips
1 quart/1 liter white
wine vinegar

With their beautiful deep orange–red fruit, rose bushes bring dashes of glorious color to hedgerows in the fall, but they are also rich in other ways. Rose hip vinegar with a drop of honey is delicious on fruit salads.

■ Wash and dry the rose hips and remove the seeds—a rather laborious job but well worth doing.

■ Layer the rose hips in a nonreactive bowl, pour over the vinegar, and let steep in a warm, dry place for 4 weeks.

■ Strain the liquid through a cheesecloth or muslin cloth and transfer to sterilized bottles. Tightly sealed, rose hip vinegar will keep for 2–3 months.

GIFT
INSPIRATION

Attach a thin strip of paper to the bottles with information about the contents, the expiration date, and some serving suggestions.

Eggnog

A little eggnog goes down well at most times of the year and makes a more unusual but useful gift. It can be enjoyed on its own or in desserts. Make an extra bottle to keep for yourself!

■ Beat or whisk the egg yolks with the sugar until light and fluffy; make sure all the sugar has dissolved. Pour in the cream in a thin stream and mix until smooth and silky.

■ Continue to beat at low speed and gradually add the rum or brandy.

■ Transfer the eggnog to sterilized bottles and seal tightly. Stored in a cool, dry place, eggnog will keep for up to 2 months.

TIP

Use the egg whites to make meringues and they can be given as gifts, too.

Mocha Liqueur

INGREDIENTS

1 vanilla bean
5 cloves
2 sticks of cinnamon
Scant 2⅔ quarts/
3 liters milk
1⅓ cups/300 ml
strong brewed
espresso coffee
Sugar to taste
3 cups/700 ml vodka
1 pinch of nutmeg

This is a very tasty liqueur, especially for those coffee lovers who appreciate the flavor of mocha, enhanced with more than a little dash of alcohol.

▓ Add the scraped-out seeds from the vanilla bean, the cloves, and the cinnamon sticks to the milk and bring to a boil.

▓ Let cool and add the espresso and the sugar. Pour in the vodka and season the mixture with nutmeg.

▓ Strain the liqueur through a cheesecloth or muslin cloth and transfer to sterilized bottles. Stored in a cool, dry place, the liqueur will keep for about 2 months.

VARIATION

You can replace the milk with the same volume of vodka to make a clear mocha liqueur.

Mulled Wine
Spice Mixture

5 star anise
1 stick of cinnamon
Handful each of
dried hibiscus
flowers, sloes, and
rose hip peel
10 cloves
Grated zest of
1 unwaxed orange

This mixture is a magical idea for the holiday season. With some pretty wrapping, it will bring warmth and a smile to chilly days.

▇ Crumble the star anise and the cinnamon stick and mix with the dried ingredients and the cloves.

▇ Place the orange zest and the spice mixture in clean glass jars with lids.

TIP

You can vary the spice mixture by adding a few cardamom pods.

Baked
Apple Jam

INGREDIENTS

7 lb 11 oz/3.5 kg
apples
2 sticks of cinnamon
Oil for brushing
Granulated sugar (for
coating the apples)
5½ cups/1.2 kg jam
sugar
2 tbsp lemon juice
1 cup/100 g shelled
walnuts
Ground cinnamon,
to taste

▓ Preheat the oven to 390°F/200°C. Wash and core the apples using a corer and insert a stick of cinnamon in two of them. Brush all the apples with oil, roll them in the granulated sugar, and place them on a cookie sheet.

▓ Bake the apples in the preheated oven for about 45 minutes until they are nice and soft. Remove the cinnamon sticks, crush the apples to a puree in a bowl, and pass through a strainer.

▓ Bring the apple puree to a boil in a pan with the jam sugar and lemon juice. While the jam is cooking, briefly dry-fry the walnuts in a skillet, crush with a mortar and pestle, and add to the apple jam mixture.

▓ Season the jam to taste with ground cinnamon and transfer to sterilized jars while still hot. Let the sealed jars stand upside down for 5 minutes. The jam will keep for about 3–4 months.

GIFT INSPIRATION

Find out how to make the planter gift packaging on page 148.

Baked Apples in Jars

INGREDIENTS

4 small apples (to fit
in 4 small Mason/
Kilner jars)
2½ tbsp/40 g
softened butter
1½ tbsp/20 g sugar
Ground cinnamon,
to taste
3 tbsp/20 g raisins
3 tbsp/20 g chopped
almonds
Generous ¾ cup/
200 ml apple juice

These individual baked apples presented in attractive jars make
the perfect dessert gift to take to lunch or dinner parties.

■ Wash the apples, carefully slice off the tops with the stalks
using a knife, and set aside. Core the apples using a corer and
place them in sterilized jars. Mix the butter with the sugar, cinnamon, raisins, and almonds and stuff the apples with the mixture.
Replace the reserved apple "lids" and pour over the apple juice.
Seal the jars. The bottled apples should be baked before serving.

■ If you prefer to cook the apples before bottling, bake them
in an ovenproof dish in a preheated oven at 390°F/200°C for
20 minutes, or until the apples are cooked through. Let cool, place
in sterilized jars, and seal the lids tightly. The apples will keep for
2–3 months in a cool place.

TIP

Tender apples like
Granny Smith are
especially suitable
for baking.

Cakes in Jars

INGREDIENTS

14 tbsp/200 g
butter plus extra for
greasing
4 eggs
Scant 1 cup/200 g
brown sugar
Scant 2¼ cups/
300 g all-purpose
(plain) flour
2 tsp baking powder
7 tbsp/50 g ground
almonds
Chocolate sprinkles,
to taste
Bread crumbs for
the jars

These cute cakes presented in attractive glass jars offer a charming alternative to a larger version and make tasty family treats.

▒ Preheat the oven to 390°F/200°C. Melt the butter and let it cool. While it is cooling, cream the eggs and sugar until light and fluffy.

▒ Mix the flour with the baking powder and stir into the butter mixture, alternating it with spoonfuls of the ground almonds. Fold in the chocolate sprinkles.

▒ Grease the jars, sprinkle them with the bread crumbs, and fill with the cake batter. Bake in the preheated oven for about 45 minutes.

▒ Chocoholics might like to add a little unsweetened cocoa powder to the batter, and gingerbread or pumpkin pie spices will be a hit during the holiday season (see photo).

GIFT
INSPIRATION

The jars shown here
are sealed with clips
and decorated with
raffia, pine branches,
and pine cones
sprayed silver.

Cupcakes with Berry Cream

TIP

The cupcakes look really pretty when baked in paper cases in matching colors. These are widely available in stores in various sizes (see photo left).

INGREDIENTS

8½ tbsp/125 g softened butter, plus extra for greasing
Scant 1½ cups/200 g all-purpose (plain) flour
3 eggs
1½ tsp baking powder
⅔ cup/150 g super-fine (caster) sugar
¼ cup /60 ml milk
1 tsp vanilla extract
2½ cups/9 oz /250 g fresh raspberries, blackberries, or strawberries
1 cup/150 g crème fraîche or heavy cream
1 tbsp confectioners' (icing) sugar
Sugar or marzipan flowers

What's not to love? Small, sensational mouthfuls that are gone in two bites and leave you and your friends wanting more …

■ Preheat the oven to 360°F/180°C. Beat together the butter, flour, eggs, baking powder, sugar, milk, and vanilla to make a smooth batter.

■ Distribute the batter among greased muffin cases, filling them about three quarters full. Bake the cakes in the preheated oven for 18–20 minutes. Let cool.

■ To make the frosting, wash the berries and crush lightly with a fork to form a puree. Stir the crème fraîche or cream into the berries and work in the sugar to make a smooth cream.

■ Using a teaspoon, remove a small piece from the top of each cupcake, fill the hole with frosting and decorate the top with a swirl of frosting and sugar flowers or the little piece of the cake.

Make and Bake with Your Heart

Apple and Pistachio Treats

GIFT
INSPIRATION

Present your cakes
in pretty paper
cupcake cases.

INGREDIENTS

2¼ lb/1 kg cooking
apples
Juice of 1 lemon
2¾ cups/600 g sugar
(approx.)
Scraped-out seeds
from 1 vanilla bean
1¼ cups/150 g
pistachios
Oil for your hands

These treats are both delicious and decorative. Pop a few in a
pretty gift box for the perfect present.

▓ Peel, core, and chop the apples, then drizzle with the lemon
juice. Slowly bring to a boil with 7 tbsp (100 ml) water and cook
for about 30 minutes until soft and fluffy.

▓ Pass the apple mixture through a strainer, add the same quantity of sugar (about 2¾ cups/1¼ lb/600 g) and the vanilla seeds,
and simmer for around 1 hour, stirring frequently. The mixture
should be very sticky.

▓ Chop the pistachios coarsely and scatter over a cookie sheet
lined with baking parchment. Lightly oil your hands and shape
the cooled apple mixture into balls before rolling them in the
chopped pistachios.

▓ Let dry overnight. The treats will keep in an airtight tin for
about 4 weeks.

Apple and Hazelnut Crispbread

GIFT
INSPIRATION

Wrap the crispbread
in pretty sandwich
wrappers and
present it in a small
wooden tray. Tie with
some twine and it's
ready to take to
your friends.

INGREDIENTS

9 oz/250 g dried
apple rings
½ cup/70 g
hazelnuts
1 oz/25 g fresh yeast
1¼ cups/300 ml
lukewarm milk
Salt
1⅔ cups/250 g
spelt flour
Generous ¾ cup/
120 g toasted whole
grain oat flour

This crunchy crispbread is the perfect accompaniment for a cheeseboard. No dry and dull crispbread here, this recipe delivers both taste and crunch!

■ Preheat the oven to 430°F/220°C. Chop the apple rings finely and the hazelnuts coarsely.

■ Stir the yeast into the lukewarm milk, adding the salt, both types of flour, the hazelnuts, and the apple. Work into a soft dough; if it gets too sticky, add a little more spelt flour.

■ Lightly flour your counter, roll out the dough, and cut into 20 pieces. Place the pieces on a lined cookie sheet and bake in the preheated oven for 6–7 minutes.

■ Reduce the heat to 120°F/50°C and leave the crispbread to bake for another hour with the oven door ajar. Let cool on a wire rack.

Marzipan Pastries

INGREDIENTS

7 oz /200 g
marzipan
6 tbsp/80 g
confectioners' (icing)
sugar
²/₃ cup/80 g ground
almonds
1 egg, separated
2 tbsp all-purpose
(plain) flour
1 tbsp orange
liqueur
1½ oz/40 g shelled
almonds
4 tbsp milk

These pastries—known as Bethmännchen in their native Germany—come from the Frankfurt area and are probably named after the Bethmann family. The pastry originally featured four almond halves, representing the family's four sons, but one piece was removed following the death of one of the sons, named Heinrich.

■ Chop the marzipan coarsely and place in a bowl. Sift in the sugar and stir in the ground almonds, egg white, flour, and orange liqueur. Knead the mixture to form a dough.

■ Preheat the oven to 350°F/175°C. Make small balls of the dough and decorate each with three almond halves.

■ Whisk the egg yolk with the milk and glaze the pastries. Place on a lined cookie sheet and bake in the preheated oven for about 15 minutes. Let cool on a wire rack.

GIFT
INSPIRATION

Place the small pastries in a cardboard box, with another box upside down on top to form a simple lid. Tie together with a length of cord or twine.

Muesli Cookies

½ cup/100 g brown
sugar
¼ cup/50 g white
sugar
1 egg
8½ tbsp/125 g butter
Scant 1¾ cups/170 g
all-purpose (plain)
flour
½ tsp baking soda
¼ cup/75 g oatmeal
½ cup/40 g dried
apple rings
⅓ cup/50 g each
dried apricots, dried
coconut pieces and
golden raisins
½ tsp ground
cinnamon

These crunchy cookies are both delectable and delightful, especially when presented in a simple yet stylish bag.

■ Cream the brown and white sugars with the egg and the softened butter until soft and creamy peaks are formed. Gradually fold in the flour, baking soda, oatmeal, diced dried fruit, coconut, golden raisins, and cinnamon. Work into a smooth dough.

■ Preheat the oven to 350°F/175°C. Make small balls of the dough and arrange on a lined cookie sheet. Flatten them down slightly and bake for 18–20 minutes until the cookies are golden brown. Remove from oven and leave on cookie sheet for a few minutes to firm up before transferring to a wire rack to cool completely.

GIFT
INSPIRATION

Make some simple but effective packaging by using crimping shears to cut a hole in one side of some white paper bags. Tape a clear plastic sheet behind the hole to make a transparent window.

Vanillekipferl

INGREDIENTS

10 tbsp/140 g
softened butter
7 tbsp/100 g
superfine (caster)
sugar
2 vanilla beans
2 egg yolks
1⅓ cups/200 g
all-purpose (plain)
flour
Generous ¾ cup/
100 g ground
almonds
1½ tsp/20 g
confectioners' (icing)
sugar

These delicious half-moon cookies are a German classic for the Christmas season. Few can resist the delicate flavor of these tasty vanilla treats as they melt in the mouth.

■ Whisk the butter to a foam with a hand mixer or blender. Stir in the sugar and the scraped-out seeds of 1 vanilla bean. Fold in the egg yolks and beat the mixture until it is light and creamy.

■ Fold in the flour and ground almonds. Flour your hands, and form the dough into three sausages, each ¾ inch/2 cm in diameter. Wrap in foil and chill in the refrigerator for 1 hour.

■ Preheat the oven to 360°F/180°C. Cut the dough into slices about the width of a finger and form them into small crescents. Place on a lined cookie sheet and bake for about 12 minutes (the cookies should not brown).

■ Mix the confectioners' sugar with the scraped-out seeds of the second vanilla bean and roll the cookies in the mixture after letting them cool a little.

Butter Heart Cookies

1¾ cups/250 g
all-purpose (plain)
flour
1 cup + 2 tbsp/
250 g confectioners'
(icing) sugar
Grated zest of
1 lemon
1 egg
⅔ cup/150 g cold
butter, cut into small
pieces
Blue food coloring
½ tbsp lemon juice

People of all ages like cookie-cutter cookies. They are so easy to decorate creatively, whether with sprinkles, frosting (icing), or sugar flowers. These look very professional.

▓ Make a pastry dough with the flour, 9 tbsp/125 g of the sugar, lemon zest, egg, and butter. Wrap the dough in foil and chill in the refrigerator for 1 hour.

▓ Preheat the oven to 360°F/180°C. Roll out the dough until it is about ⅛ inch/3–4 mm thick and use heart cutters to cut out the cookies. Place the cookies on a lined cookie sheet and bake for about 10 minutes; let cool on a wire rack.

▓ Stir the food coloring and the lemon juice into the remaining sugar and glaze the cookies with the mixture before decorating them in your chosen design.

VARIATION

Tiny dots of white frosting make these hearts look really cute.

Chocolate Truffles

VARIATION

For a nonalcoholic version, make some light truffles with 2 tbsp/10 g ground hazelnuts, or add a touch of ground cardamom. Roll the truffles in confectioners' sugar, crushed nuts, or chocolate flakes.

INGREDIENTS

3½ oz/100 g semi-sweet chocolate
3 oz/80 g sweet cream butter
6 tbsp/80 g confectioners' (icing) sugar
4 tsp/20 ml cognac

Make twice as many as you think you need because you won't be able to resist these buttery truffles! You'll have eaten half of them before it's even time to hand them over as a present.

■ Melt the chocolate in a bowl set over a pan of simmering water (do not allow the bowl to come in contact with the water). Let cool slightly. Cream the butter and sugar together and then gradually add the chocolate, one spoonful at a time, before finally stirring in the cognac.

■ Shape the truffle mixture into nut-sized portions, roll in cocoa powder, and place in praline cases.

■ The pralines will keep for at least 1 week in the refrigerator if you can resist eating them before then.

GIFT INSPIRATION

Arrange three truffles in a papier-mâché pebble box, as shown on page 162.

Chocolate Candy Lollipops with Spices

When dunked in hot milk, these homemade chocolate candy lollipops turn into a wonderful chocolate drink, and you can even spice up your coffee with them.

◼ Bring the cream, vanilla seeds, and spices to a boil. Remove the pan from the heat and put to one side.

◼ Chop the chocolate finely and melt in a bowl set over a pan of simmering water (do not allow the bowl to come in contact with the water). Stir in the spiced cream a little at a time to form a smooth mixture.

◼ Pour the mixture into the small plastic molds. Place a plastic spoon in each one and let cool.

◼ Decorate with chocolate sprinkles or coat in a layer of white chocolate for an extra chocolatey flavor.

VARIATION

A pinch of chili powder will give these chocolate candy lollipops an unmistakable kick, and the alcoholic version (with an added 10 tbsp/ 5½ oz/150 g cream and 3½ tbsp/50 ml rum) is one you won't easily forget.

INGREDIENTS

Generous ¾ cup/
200 g light (single)
cream
Scraped-out seeds of
1 vanilla bean
Ground cinnamon
to taste
Ground cardamom
to taste
11 oz/300 g semi-
sweet, milk, or white
chocolate
Plastic molds
Plastic spoons

Cornflake Chocolate

INGREDIENTS

7 oz/200 g milk chocolate
3½ oz/100 g semi-sweet chocolate
scant 1½ cups/ 35 g cornflakes
Chocolate mold or foil

You can vary the base chocolate used to make this delicious cornflake chocolate according to personal taste. Use milk or semisweet chocolate, or a mixture of both.

■ Break the chocolate into chunks and melt in a bowl set over a pan of simmering water (do not allow the bowl to come in contact with the water).

■ Crush the cornflakes in a plastic bag. Pour as much of the melted chocolate as you wish into a chocolate mold (or make a pool of the chocolate on a piece of foil), mix the cornflakes with the remaining chocolate, and sprinkle over the top of the slightly cooled chocolate to form a coating.

VARIATION

Versions made with white chocolate, a mixture of muesli, nuts, or pieces of broken cookies are all delicious.

Pine Nut Chocolate

INGREDIENTS

¼ cup/30 g pine nuts
2 sprigs rosemary
11 oz/300 g milk chocolate
Chocolate mold or foil

■ Dry-fry the pine nuts briefly in a skillet and let cool. Strip the rosemary leaves from the stalks and chop finely.

■ Coarsely chop the chocolate and melt in a bowl set over a pan of simmering water (do not allow the bowl to come in contact with the water). Pour the melted chocolate into a chocolate mold (or make a pool of the chocolate on a piece of foil), let cool slightly, then scatter the nuts and the rosemary over the top.

VARIATION

You can dye white chocolate bright green with food coloring, or mix it with strawberry puree to make pink chocolate, which sets off green pistachios nicely. You can also use almonds or hazelnuts as an alternative.

Happy Valentine's Day!

Europeans have celebrated St. Valentine's Day (February 14) for only a few centuries, but "Lovers' Day" has a longer tradition in the English-speaking world, where people have been sending flowers and love letters to the object of their affections since as long ago as the 15th century. Nowadays, we give our friends and loved-ones all kinds of small gifts, and heart-shaped ones are among the most popular.

Made with Wool, Thread, and Love

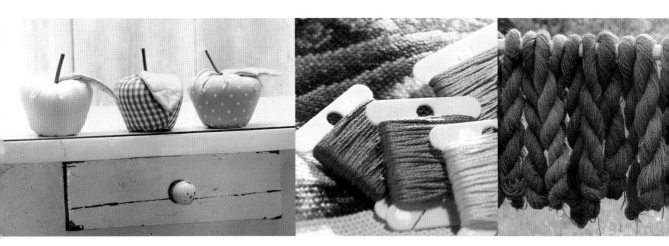

What could be nicer than receiving a handcrafted gift, carefully chosen, or lovingly knitted, crocheted, sewn, or felted. My selection of craft projects is designed to be as unique and personal as possible. As you make each one, you may think of the friend or family member for whom it is intended and wonder if it will fit, if the color will suit them, or if the materials will be soft enough. There may be plenty of things to consider before you start making an item, but there will be no doubt at all about the final result: these gifts are all quick and easy to make, they don't have to be perfect, and their rustic charm is sure to be a big hit.

Handy Fingerless Gloves

Bring on winter! These stylish gloves will keep your hands cozy and fashionably warm.

■ For the right glove, cast on 29 stitches. Divide stitches between 3 double-pointed needles, and join in a round. Knit 3 rounds of knit 1, purl 1 ribbing. For the next round, knit 16, purl 2, knit 9 for the cable, purl 2, to complete the round. To make the first cable twist: knit 16, purl 2, slip the next 3 stitches onto the cable needle and take to the back, knit across the next 3 stitches, knit the 3 stitches from the cable needle, knit 3, purl 2.

■ Following the pattern, work 3 straight rounds. For the next cable twist: knit 16, purl 2, knit 3, slip the next 3 stitches onto the cable needle and bring to the front, knit 3, knit the 3 stitches from the cable needle, purl 2.

■ The cable twists are worked alternately after every 3 straight rounds. Following the pattern, work until the piece measures 9 inches/23 cm. On the next round, after completing the cable stitches, purl 2, knit 2, then take the next 5 stitches onto a safety pin. On the next round cast the 5 stitches back on and carry on working rounds in pattern until the piece measures 11 inches/28 cm. Cast off loosely.

■ Take the stitches from the safety pin onto one of the double-pointed needles, pick up the 5 cast-on stitches, and knit across the 10 stitches in a round for 1½ inches/4 cm in stockinette stitch. Cast off loosely. Sew in yarn ends carefully with the darning needle.

■ Work the left glove in the same way but reverse the pattern. The stitches for the thumbhole in the left glove are 11 stitches (purl 2, knit 9) after the cable pattern.

MATERIALS

2 balls (4 oz/100 g) Lang Yarns Malou super chunky yarn (70% alpaca, 20% polyamide, 10% new wool; length/weight 71 yds/65 m per 50 g) in gray
4 double-pointed knitting needles, size 10½ (7mm)
Cable needle
Safety pin
Darning needle

GIFT INSPIRATION

Once you have decorated the gloves with a nostalgic heart-shaped gift tag and a ribbon tied in a bow, the gloves will be ready for their grand entrance.

Giant Snuggly Scarf

TENSION GAUGE

11 stockinette
stitches to 4 inches/
10 cm

SIZE OF FINISHED SCARF

Length: 102 inches/
260 cm
Width: 22 inches/
56 cm

MATERIALS

10 balls (20 oz/500 g)
Lang Yarns Malou
super chunky yarn
(70% alpaca, 20%
polyamide, 10% new
wool; length/weight
71 yds/65 m per
50 g) in gray
Knitting needles,
size 10½ (7mm)
Cable needle
Darning needle

Inkeri (shown above) looks absolutely delighted with her lovely, homemade gift.

▦ Cast on 62 stitches and work 2 inches/5 cm knit 1, purl 1 ribbing. For the cable pattern, work the stitches as follows: 1 selvedge stitch, knit 2, purl 6, knit 4 (narrow cable), purl 5, knit 6 (wide cable), purl 5, knit 4 (narrow cable), purl 5, knit 6 (wide cable), purl 5, knit 4 (narrow cable), purl 6, knit 2, 1 selvedge stitch.

▦ Following the pattern, the narrow cable twists (over 4 stitches) are worked every 6 rows, and the wide cable twists (over 6 stitches) are worked every 12 rows. The stitches are otherwise knitted according to the pattern.

▦ To make the cable twists, slip the first 2 stitches (3 stitches for the wide cables) onto the cable needle and bring to the front, knit the next 2 stitches (3 stitches for the wide cable) and then knit the stitches from the cable needle.

▦ Continue in pattern until the scarf measures 100 inches/ 255 cm, then work the last 2 inches/5 cm in knit 1, purl 1 ribbing. Cast off loosely. Sew in the ends of the yarn carefully with the darning needle.

Snug Snood

■ Cast on 63 stitches and work in pattern as follows: purl 3, knit 2 (cable 1), purl 2, knit 6 (cable 2), purl 2, knit 4 (cable 3), purl 2, knit 9 (cable 4), purl 2, knit 8 (cable 5), purl 2, knit 4 (cable 6), purl 2, knit 12 (cable 7), purl 3. Knit the stitches as they appear on the reverse rows. The piece is knitted straight, without any increases or decreases.

■ For cable 1, twist the stitches every 2 rows.

■ For cable 2 (every 6 rows), slip the first 3 stitches onto the cable needle and take to the back, knit 3, then knit across the 3 stitches from the cable needle.

■ For cable 3 (every 6 rows), slip the first 2 stitches onto the cable needle and take to the back, knit 2, then knit across the 2 stitches from the cable needle.

■ For cable 4 (three-plait cable), slip the first 3 stitches onto the cable needle and bring to the front, knit 3, then knit across the 3 stitches from the cable needle, knit 3. After 6 rows straight, knit 3, slip the next 3 stitches onto the cable needle and take them to the back, knit 3, then knit across the 3 stitches from the cable needle. Repeat the entire process after a further 6 rows.

■ For cable 5 (every 4 rows), slip the first 2 stitches onto the cable needle and bring to the front, knit 2, then knit the 2 stitches from the cable needle. Slip the next 2 stitches onto the cable needle and take to the back, knit 2, then knit across the stitches from the cable needle.

■ For cable 6, as cable 3.

■ For cable 7, as cable 3 but every 12 rows.

■ Work the piece in the cable pattern until it is approx. 40 inches/ 100 cm; the width of your shoulders will determine how long the piece needs to be. Sew up the seam. Cast on 12 stitches and knit approx. 8 inches/20 cm stockinette stitch. Sew this strip around to hide the seam and sew in the yarn ends with a darning needle.

MATERIALS

6 oz/150 g cream cashmere yarn (100% cashmere, 8-ply; length/weight 142 yds/130 m per 50 g) in ecru
Knitting needles, size 13 (9mm)
Cable needle
Darning needle

SIZE OF FINISHED SNOOD

Length: approx. 40 inches/100 cm
Width: approx. 10½ inches/26 cm

TIP

If you prefer, you can knit cable (no. 2) in the strip that covers the seam.

Pretty Knitted Bags

TENSION GAUGE

11 stockinette
stitches to 4 inches/
10 cm, using
doubled yarn

BRIOCHE STITCH

Row 1: knit 1, purl 1
alternately.
Row 2: *knit 1, bring
yarn forward, slip 1
purlwise, bring yarn
over right needle,
repeat from * to
end of row.
Row 3: *knit 1
together with its
paired yarnover,
bring yarn forward,
slip 1 purlwise, bring
yarn over right
needle, repeat from *
to end of row.
Repeat row 3 until
you reach the
desired length.

MATERIALS

10 balls (20 oz/500 g)
SMC Select Extra Soft
Merino (100%
Merino wool; length/
weight 142 yds/
130 m per 50 g) in
gray or dark brown
Knitting needles,
size 10½ (7mm)
Cable needle
2 double-pointed
knitting needles, size
10½ (7mm)
Darning needle
1 zipper, 19 inches/
47 cm long
20 inches/50 cm
lining fabric in a
matching color

Young girls in particular will adore this fun accessory. Your gift is in the bag.

■ Using doubled yarn, cast on 55 stitches and work 3½ inches/ 9 cm of stockinette stitch. For the cable pattern, work as follows: 1 selvedge stitch, *knit 1, purl 1, knit 1, purl 1, knit 1, purl 2, knit 1, purl 1, knit 1, purl 1, knit 1, purl 1, knit 1, purl 2, repeat from * to end of row. Apart from the purl 2 on either side of each of the cables, all the stitches in subsequent rows are knitted in brioche stitch (see instructions, right).

■ Follow the pattern for 16 rows (3¼ inches/8 cm), then work the 3 cable twists (over 7 stitches). To do this, slip the first 4 stitches onto the cable needle and take them to the back, knit the remaining 3 stitches (an uneven number of stitches, otherwise the brioche stitch cannot be cabled), then work the stitches from the cable needle in pattern. Continue until the piece measures 31 inches/80 cm, then work a further 3½ inches/9 cm stockinette stitch and cast off loosely.

■ Fold the piece in half and sew up the side seams. To make a cord, cast on 3 stitches onto a double-pointed needle using 4 strands of yarn. Knit 1 row, then slide the stitches to the other end of the needle. Knit the next row without turning, pulling the yarn tight across the back of your stitches to create a rounded cord. Continue until the cord measures 39 inches/1 m. Fold over the top stockinette section and stitch in place. Line the bag with fabric and sew in the zipper. Finally, fold the cord in half and attach to the bag.

Knitted Mug Cozy

Make your tea, hot chocolate, or coffee look as good as they taste with these pretty cup and mug warmers.

■ Cast on 48 stitches and, for the cable pattern, purl 8, knit 4 (cable), purl 10, knit 4 (cable) purl 10, knit 4 (cable), purl 8. The reverse rows are always knitted as the stitches appear.

■ Row 3: for the cable twists, slip the purl stitch before the cable stitches onto the cable needle, take to the back and knit the first 2 cable stitches. Purl the stitch from the cable needle, slip the next 2 stitches onto the cable needle, bring them to the front, purl the next stitch, knit the two stitches from the cable needle.

■ Rows 5 and 7: knit the stitches as they appear.

■ Row 9: for the cable twists, slip the first 2 knit stitches onto the cable needle and take to the back, purl 1, knit the 2 stitches from the cable needle. Slip the next purl stitch onto the cable needle, bring it to the front and knit the next 2 stitches, then purl the stitch from the cable needle.

■ Row 11: for the cable twists, slip the first 2 knit stitches onto the cable needle, take to the back, knit the next 2 stitches and then knit the stitches from the cable needle. The cabling is repeated once more from row 4.

■ Cast off loosely, sew up the seam and carefully sew in the yarn ends with a darning needle.

■ The number of stitches and the pattern are the same for the gray cup cover, as is the cabling in principle. The cabling is worked as described above over 4 stitches after the first 2 rows. However, the cable is twisted again after row 4, and then 2 cable twists are repeated over 2 rows, as at the beginning. The pattern is finished off with the double cabling.

Materials

1 ball (2 oz/50 g) GGH Maxima (100% Merino wool; length/weight 121 yds/110 m per 50 g) each in gray, natural, and white
Knitting needles, size 6 (4 mm)
Cable needle
Darning needle
Cup or mug (straight sides rather than curved)

Tension gauge

18 stitches and 22 rows will give a 4-inch/10-cm square

Size

Adapt the size of the cozy to fit your cups.

Knitted Love Hearts

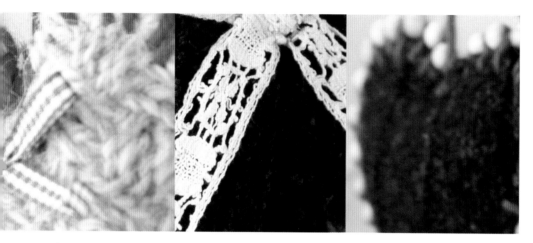

SIZE OF
FINISHED HEARTS

Height: 6 inches/
15 cm
Width: 4½ inches/
12 cm

MATERIALS

Old knitted sweaters
or socks
Large pins
Fiberfill
Red knitting yarn
Lace braid or ribbons
Wooden beads

This project involves cutting and stitching but no knitting, so it will be finished in no time and look great. The hearts are made from old, preloved knitted items or pieces of knitting in which you made a few mistakes.

■ Cut pairs of hearts of different sizes from the old knitted items. Pin the pairs together, leaving a small opening.

■ Fill the the hearts with a small amount of fiberfill before sewing all around the edges with the red yarn in blanket stitch (see page 166) .

■ Decorate the finished hearts with a braid or ribbon bow, or sew wooden beads around the edge, and add a small loop of red yarn for hanging.

Fringed Scarf

Materials

4 oz/100 g
cashmere yarn
(100% cashmere,
4-ply; length/weight
200 m/220 yds per
50 g)
Crochet hook,
size H/8 (5 mm)
Darning needle

This scarf is quick to make and looks great teamed with a cozy sweater. The soft cashmere wool is the next best thing to giving someone a warm hug.

■ Using the crochet hook, make a length of chain stitches 71 inches/180 cm long.

■ Work a loop of 20 chain stitches and 1 single crochet into each of the chain stitches along the entire length. To finish, carefully tie off the yarn and sew in the ends.

And the scarf is done! It's such a quick job, you could crochet a pretty accessory for a friend next.

NB The same terms are used in the US and UK to describe different crochet stitches. We use US crochet terms throughout. For UK terms: single crochet = double crochet; double crochet = treble; triple crochet = double treble.

Size

Length: approx.
71 inches/80 cm

Spiral Scarf

MATERIALS

4 oz/100 g
cashmere yarn
(100% cashmere,
4-ply; length/weight
200 m/220 yds per
50 g)
Crochet hook,
size H/8 (5 mm)
Darning needle

This fun scarf rolls up like a corkscrew and makes a real fashion statement.

▨ Using the crochet hook, make a length of chain stitches 71 inches/180 cm long. Work to the following pattern:

▨ Row 1 (singles): work a row of single crochet stitches into every chain along the entire length.

▨ Row 2 (doubles): work a row of double crochet stitches along the entire length, working 2 doubles into every second stitch.

▨ Row 3 (triples): (i.e. doubles with 2 yarn overs), work a row of triple crochet stitches, *working 2 triples in each stitch 5 times in a row, then working 1 triple into the hole between the stitches on the previous row. Repeat continuously from *.

▨ Row 4 (double triples): (i.e. doubles with 3 yarn overs), work a row of double triple crochet stitches along the entire length, working 2 double triples into every second stitch. Tie off the yarn and sew in the ends.

Advent Wool

This advent calendar for knitters is a charming gift to make for the days leading up to the holiday season. Hide small gift items in the balls of wool as extra Christmas surprises.

▓ Wind the wool around the 24 surprise gifts and arrange them in a pretty basket or attractive bowl with the knitting needles.

▓ Write the numbers 1 to 24 on the stars, glue the stars to the toothpicks, and place in the balls of wool. The knitter has to use up the wool in order to access the surprise. Cheating by simply unraveling the balls is not allowed!

TIP

You will find ideas for homemade baskets on page 138 (Newspaper Basket) and page 134 (Stylish Popsicle Stick Basket).

Crochet Flowers

MATERIALS

Odds and ends of
wool in lavender
blue and white
Crochet hook,
size E/4 (3.5 mm)
Darning needle

■ Using lavender yarn, crochet a ring of 3 chain stitches. For the foundation row, work 10 single crochet stitches into the center of the ring, joining the last stitch to the first with a slip stitch.

■ For the first flower petal, work 3 chain stitches, then work 2 single crochet stitches into the center stitch of the chain you have just made. Skip a stitch and work a single crochet stitch into the foundation row. Work 3 more chain stitches for the next petal, then 2 single crochet stitches into the center stitch of the chain you have just made. Carry on in this way until all 5 petals are completed. Tie off the yarn with a slip stitch and sew in the ends.

■ Using the white yarn, work 2 chain stitches with a long starting thread and join with a slip stitch to form a small bobble. Leave a long thread as an end thread. Pull the bobbles through the center of the flowers and use the thread ends to tie the flowers to the branches.

VARIATION

Decorate a flowerpot with some matching fabric, braid, and leftover wool.

Felt Mouse in the House

Materials

Wool batting in gray
Olive oil soap
Foam rubber
White vinegar
Pink leather cord for a tail
Beige and pink felt fabric
4 white and 4 black beads
Brown sewing thread
Horsehair
Sewing needle
Scissors

Furry mice are not allowed in the kitchen, but these funny felt finger puppets should be welcome!

▓ Cut a triangle of foam 2¾ inches/7 cm high and 1½ inches/4 cm wide (at the base). Pull the batting apart into small clumps. Make a soapy mixture with the soap and water, as hot as possible. Place a layer of the wool batting over the foam and moisten with water. Add another layer at right angles to the first, moisten, and repeat the process until you have built up about 5 or 6 layers of wool.

▓ Sprinkle soapy water over the layers and gently stroke the surface. When you can no longer feel the surface fibers moving, press harder until the fibers hold together. Keep felting all over the surface using pressure and soapy water until no individual strands come loose, and then press out as much of the liquid as possible. Turn over, fold over the rough edges, and repeat the process.

▓ Remove the foam rubber, fold in rough edges at the base, and felt these until they are solid. Rinse out the soap using clean water and adding a dash of vinegar to the last few rinses.

▓ When dry, sew on the small leather tail; cut 2 ears from the felt fabric, and sew on. Add the white beads for teeth and the black beads for eyes, then embroider a nose with the thread and attach horsehair whiskers.

Lovable Sheep

MATERIALS

Wool batting in
white and brown
Olive oil soap
1 styrofoam egg,
approx. 1¼ inches by
1½ inches/3 cm by
4 cm, for the head
White felt fabric
1 styrofoam ball
4 inches/10 cm in
diameter, for the
body
Sewing needle
Glue
Scissors

Peeping out of the gift box with its head cocked slightly to one side, this cuddly sheep can't wait to meet its new owner.

■ To make the head, pull the white wool batting into clumps and cover the styrofoam egg in layers, arranging each layer at right angles to the previous one. Saturate the wool with hot, soapy water and roll the egg around between the palms of your hands without squeezing, until the fibers stick together. Once the egg has been completely felted (about 10 minutes), create the eyes, nose, and mouth by working in strips of the brown wool batting with your fingertips. Rinse with clean, cold water and leave to dry.

■ Cut 2½-inch/6-cm wide strips from the white felt fabric, fold them in half lengthwise, and make ½-inch/1-cm deep cuts in the folds at intervals of approx. ½ inch/1 cm to make loops.

■ Cut out 2 ovals of felt fabric about ¾ inch/2 cm high for the ears and sew these onto the dried head. Make a circular crown from a 4-inch/10-cm strip of the felt fabric and glue it on.

■ To make the body, flatten the styrofoam ball on one side. Starting at the bottom, glue on the folded felt strips in a spiral, working round the body and leaving a space free at the top to glue on the head.

Heartfelt with Felt

Charming Felt Pumps

These delightful felt slippers are seamless and made to fit perfectly. Add a red bow and you have pretty, perfect pumps.

▓ Using a ballpoint pen, draw a template for the slippers on the bubble wrap. The template should be for the sole of the foot, with a shrinkage allowance of about 2 inches/5 cm. Cut out the template and make a copy for the second shoe.

▓ Place the template on a sheet of bubble wrap. Pull the wool batting into clumps with dry fingers and build up layers of the dark gray batting on the template, arranging each layer at right angles to the previous one; don't worry if the wool overlaps the template, it will be folded over to the reverse side.

▓ Using the dish scrubber, dampen the wool with the soapy water, press it down with your hand, and gently stroke the surface. When you can no longer feel the surface fibers moving, press harder until the fibers hold together. Keep felting all over the surface using pressure and soapy water until none of the individual strands come loose. Now build up 5–6 layers of natural wool batting and work them in the same fashion. Turn over the template, fold in the overlapping wool, and repeat the same process on the other side first with the gray then the natural batting. Make the second slipper in the same way.

▓ When both pumps have been covered with a good layer of felt, cut a circular hole toward the back and remove the bubble wrap template. Roll each slipper in turn in a towel and press out the moisture. Repeat this process several times, changing the position of the shoe each time, until all the moisure has been removed. Mold the shoe to its final shape on your foot or on a shoe last.

▓ Neaten the edges around the top of the slipper with crimping shears and create a decorative border by working in strips of the red wool batting with your fingertips and felting it onto the edge.

▓ Rinse in clean water with a dash of vinegar—this will give a nice shine and make the colors stand out. To finish, when dry, cut a length of satin ribbon, tie a little bow, and sew it to the front.

MATERIALS

Bubble wrap
Ballpoint pen
Wool batting in dark gray, natural, and red
Hot soapy water
Dish scrubber
Terry cloth towel
White vinegar
Crimping shears
Red satin ribbon
Sewing needle
Scissors

TIP

Remember that the pumps will shrink by approximately one shoe size when dry.

Simply Beautiful

Made of simple white felt and finished with lace, these holiday season hanging decorations are a joy to hold and behold. They will look fabulously festive on any Christmas tree or used as a label for a heartfelt gift.

White felt fabric,
⅛ inch/3 mm thick
Scraps of old lace
Pearl beads
White sequins
White satin ribbon
White sewing thread
Sewing needle
Clear glue
Scissors

If you don't have any lace to hand, paper doilies will also look very pretty.

■ Cut out circles from the felt, approx. 4 inches/10 cm in diameter, or to your preferred size. Cut out scraps of lace to fit and glue them to the center of the felt circles. Decorate with a few beads or sequins, if you wish.

■ Cut a 5½-inch/14-cm length of satin ribbon, fold into a loop, and sew the ends to the top of the decoration. Glue another felt circle to the back—you can decorate one side or both.

Holiday Decorations

MATERIALS

White or cream felt
fabric, ¹⁄₁₆ inch/2 mm
thick
Sequins and beads,
or strings of small
beads in contrasting
colors
Narrow satin ribbon
in a matching color
Sewing thread
in matching or
contrasting colors
Sewing needle
Sewing machine
Glue
Scissors

These pretty decorations look really romantic but can also be used as an Advent calendar—make 24 and fill their small pockets with delicious treats.

■ Cut out the shapes shown in the illustration from the felt. Place two matching shapes together, and sew around the edges (by hand or machine), leaving two-thirds of the seam open at the top.

■ Sew or glue on the sequins, beads, and strings of beads. Be as creative as you like—you can also sew or glue a few strings of beads onto the tips of the decorations or use them as hanging loops.

■ Cut approx. 6-inch/15-cm lengths of the narrow satin ribbon and sew to either side of the tops of the decorations so that you can hang them up. Fill them with treats and little surprises of your choice.

TIP

If you'd rather not sew, use glue to stick the felt decorations together.

Beautiful Hearts

MATERIALS

Scraps of red
gingham fabric
Scraps of red and
white floral and
spotted fabric
Velvet ribbon or
braid
Zipper, 6½ inches/
17 cm) long
Basting thread
Basting needle
Red and white
sewing thread
Sewing machine
Scissors

This useful cosmetics bag will warm the heart of whoever receives it. The appliqué designs are attached with a sewing machine.

▥ Cut out 2 rectangles 8¼ inches/21 cm long and 5 inches/ 13 cm wide from the red gingham fabric. Cut out 3 hearts in two different sizes, one approx. 1¼–1½ inches/3–3.5 cm high and one a little smaller from the floral or spotted fabric.

▥ Arrange the hearts and the velvet ribbon or braid on one of the gingham rectangles, pin and baste them in place. Using a sewing machine with a tight zigzag stitch, sew around the edges of the motifs.

▥ With right sides facing, line up the rectangles, and pin the sides. Sew around three edges and turn the piece right side out. Insert the zipper, baste, and sew in.

SIZE OF
FINISHED BAG

Length: 7½ inches/
19 cm
Height: 4¼ inches/
11 cm

An Apple a Day

MATERIALS

Pink and white
gingham fabric
Light green and light
blue spotted fabric
Matching sewing
thread
Fiberfill
Green felt, about
⅛ inch/3 mm thick
Plain green fabric
(or handicraft felt)
3 small wooden
sticks for stems
Sewing machine
Sewing needle
Scissors

■ All the apples are sewn using the same method. Cut out a circle with a diameter of 2 inches/5 cm to make the base for each apple, then cut out 2 trapezoids for the sides (a trapezoid is shaped like a triangle with the top point cut off).

■ With right sides facing, sew the trapezoids together along their 4½-inch/12-cm long edges. Pin the base circle to the smaller opening and sew it on. Turn right side out and fill with fiberfill, being careful not to overstuff the apple.

■ To make the dip in the top of the apple, hand baste a row of stitches around the upper edge, pull the thread to gather the fabric, then take the needle down through the center of the apple and fasten off at the base.

■ Cut out 2 leaf shapes about 2 inches/5 cm wide and 3½ inches/ 9 cm long, one each from the felt and the green fabric. With right sides facing, place the 2 pieces together, sew around the edge leaving a small gap, turn right side out, and quilt a pattern of leaf veins. Tie the leaves onto the wooden stem and sew firmly to the center.

SIZE OF
FINISHED APPLE

Height: approx.
4 inches/10 cm

SIZE OF
TRAPEZOID

Bottom edge:
3½ inches/9 cm
Top edge: 5½ inches/
14 cm
Height: 4½ inches/
12 cm
All dimensions
include the seam
allowance.

Flower Garden Scarf

This bright and colorful scarf with its appliqué flowers is bound to turn heads. It is the perfect gift for anyone who thinks that giving friends a bunch of flowers is just too dull!

■ Cut out 18 oval petals for each end of the scarf from the scraps of floral fabric; they should be ¾ inch/2 cm long and 1¼ inches/ 3 cm wide (you will need to make 9 petals per flower). With right sides facing, place pairs of the petals together and sew around the edges, leaving the bottom edge open. Turn right sides out.

■ Cut out 2 circles of brown felt, each ¾ inch/2 cm in diameter. Place the two circles together and slip the petals between the edges. Baste in place all around, then machine sew. Make a second flower in the same way. Attach a flower to each end of the piece of spotted fabric.

■ Embroider the stems and leaves in chainstitch, using the green and red yarn. Embroider a row of cross stitches in the yellow yarn underneath and sew a button at the base of each stem.

■ With right sides facing, place the 2 pieces of fabric for the scarf together, pin, and sew around the edges, leaving a 4-inch/10-cm gap for turning. Turn right sides out and sew up the gap in the seam by hand.

MATERIALS

Scraps of floral fabric
Scraps of brown felt
Spotted and check
fabric, each piece
60 inches/150 cm
wide and 14 inches/
35 cm long
Sewing thread in a
matching color
Embroidery needle
Scraps of yarn in red,
green, and yellow
4 checked buttons
Sewing machine
Scissors

TIP

If you want to make the gift even more personal, and you have the time and inclination, you can appliqué an entire meadow of button flowers along the ends of the scarf.

Bath and Beauty Homemade Gifts

Wellness centers and spas are becoming increasingly popular in these hectic times, as more and more people yearn for a return to a simpler life and natural products. The projects in this section make lovely, personal gifts—your friends and family will be thrilled with creams you have mixed specially for them, bath salts infused with their favorite scents, soap made with flowers from your garden or balcony, or a massage oil made with St. John's wort for blissful relaxation. Each recipe is easy to make and will be a delight to receive in its pretty wrapping. Simply wonderful.

Lavender Soap

INGREDIENTS

Generous 1 lb/500 g
unscented raw
glycerine soap
10 drops lavender oil
1–2 tsp olive oil,
if required
1 cup dried lavender
flowers

MATERIALS

Mold for the soap

The scent of lavender is associated with freshness and cleanliness, so what could be better than capturing that in a soap? Quick and easy, it makes a great gift for lovers of the traditional scent. Keep the unused soaps between your towels or clothes to fill the whole room with their fragrance.

■ Cut the raw soap into chunks and melt in a bowl set over a pan of simmering water. Let cool slightly, then stir in the lavender oil. To make the soap even kinder on the skin, add a couple of teaspoons of olive oil.

■ Pour the mixture into a rectangular mold, scatter the lavender flowers on top, and press them down. Let dry.

TIP

Use different molds; small heart-shaped soaps look extremely pretty.

Bath Bombs

INGREDIENTS

1¾ oz/50 g cocoa
butter
½ oz/15 g emulsifier
3½ oz/100 g
cornstarch
6 oz/170 g citric acid
¾ lb/340 g sodium
carbonate
7 drops mandarin oil
(or any floral oil)

These gifts will bring the sweet smell of success to all your friends, young and old, male and female, and you can tailor the fragrance accordingly. Men may prefer the sharper notes of mandarin or grapefruit, while women are often more keen on floral fragrances.

■ Melt the cocoa butter in a bowl set over a pan of simmering water. Let cool slightly, then stir in the emulsifier.

■ Mix together the cornstarch, citric acid, and sodium carbonate and gradually stir into the cocoa butter in small amounts before adding the mandarin oil. Knead the mixture and form into balls.

■ Store in a dry place so that the bombs can dry out.

GIFT INSPIRATION

Present the bath bombs in a shell or a transparent cellophane bag with some dried flowers for extra effect.

Relaxing Bath Oil
with Lavender

INGREDIENTS

3½ tbsp/50 ml
almond oil
A few drops
lavender oil
2–3 dried sprigs
of lavender

MATERIALS

Sterilized bottle
Scissors

If you have a friend who likes to spend time in the tub at the end of a long day, then this relaxing oil would make the perfect treat.

▦ Mix the almond and lavender oil together and transfer to a sterilized bottle prepared in advance.

▦ Place the lavender sprigs in the bottle, trimming to fit if necessary. Add a few drops to a warm bath and luxuriate!

GIFT INSPIRATION

Wrapped in tissue paper or placed in an organza bag and decorated with a sprig of lavender, this oil makes a lovely birthday gift for female friends.

Bath Salts
with Algae

INGREDIENTS

½ cup/3½ oz/100 g
dried algae
5¼ cups/2¼ lb/1 kg
coarse sea salt
30 drops lemongrass
oil

These refreshing sachets of bath salts will detoxify, exfoliate, and energize. Wrapped in beautiful gift paper, they are bathing belles!

■ Cut 10 squares of linen, each 6 x 6 inches/15 x 15 cm in size. Mix the dried algae and sea salt together and divide among the 10 linen squares. Sprinkle a few drops of lemongrass oil over each pile of salt and algae and tie the squares into a sachet with the string.

■ Add a sachet to warm bathwater and relax. Scrub your skin with the bag to exfoliate.

MATERIALS

Linen fabric
String
Scissors

Quick 'n' Easy
Sugar Scrub

INGREDIENTS

²/₃ cup/5 oz/150 g
sugar
5 tsp coarse sea salt
²/₃ cup/150 ml olive
oil
A few drops of
essential oil (lemon
balm or lavender,
whichever you
prefer)

The ingredients for this sugar scrub are all pantry essentials, making it a great last-minute gift.

▮ Mix the sugar and sea salt in a bowl. Mix the olive oil and essential oil together, and add to the sugar and salt mixture in drops, stirring to keep the mixture smooth.

▮ Transfer the mixture to a clean glass jar. As a finishing touch, write the instructions for use on a label and attach it to the jar with raffia.

▮ Apply the sugar scrub in the shower or bath, rubbing the skin in a circular motion. Rinse off the residue with warm water.

MATERIALS

Clean glass jar
Label
Raffia

St. John's Wort Massage Oil

INGREDIENTS

½ oz/15 g fresh
St. John's wort
flowers
1 cup/250 ml
wheatgerm oil

For many people, a voucher for a relaxing massage at a salon is one of the best presents that money can buy. So you should find that this oil infused with St. John's wort is just the ticket.

■ Strip the fresh St. John's wort flowers from the stems and grind gently with a mortar and pestle.

■ Transfer the ground flowers to a clean jar with a sealable lid. Pour in the wheatgerm oil.

■ Let steep at room temperature until the oil has taken on a red hue. Strain the massage oil through a muslin cloth or cheesecloth and transfer to a clean bottle. Store in a cool and dry place.

MATERIALS

Muslin cloth or
cheesecloth
Clean bottle with
sealable lid

Foot Balm with Peppermint Oil

1¾ fl oz/50 ml
almond oil
1½ oz/40 g rich
moisturizer for dry
skin (e.g. Eucerin)
2 tsp/10 g cocoa
butter
1¼ tsp/6 g lanolin
20 drops
peppermint oil
½ tsp/2 ml glycerol
12 drops lactic acid

Do you have friends who are on their feet all day? This feet treat is the ideal gift for them, but remember to keep some for yourself!

■ Place the almond oil, moisturizer, cocoa butter, and lanolin in a bowl and melt over a pan of simmering water. Remove from the heat and stir with a small whisk until the mixture is just hand hot.

■ Stir in the peppermint oil, glycerol, and lactic acid, one after the other.

■ Transfer the still-warm balm to clean tins or jars and seal. The balm will keep for 3–4 weeks, if stored in a cool place.

MATERIALS

Small tins or jars
with lids

Soothing Winter Hand Balm

1 oz/30 g granulated
beeswax
Scant 1 oz/25 g
cocoa butter
²/₃ cup/150 ml
almond oil
10 drops lemon
essential oil
6 drops camomile
essential oil
8 drops lavender
essential oil

This rich hand cream is perfect for those who suffer from chapped skin in the chilly months.

▓ Melt the granulated beeswax in a bowl set over a pan of simmering water, add the cocoa butter and almond oil, and stir well.

▓ Place the bowl with the balm mixture to a large bowl of cold water, add the three essential oils, and stir the balm to form a cream as it cools to hand-hot.

▓ Transfer to small, clean bottles or jars with a good seal; the balm will keep for 3–4 weeks.

MATERIALS

Small, clean bottles
or jars with lids

Bright Eyes Gel

INGREDIENTS

1 tsp gelling agent
(e.g. Tylopur C 600)
4 tsp/20 ml distilled
water
6 drops D-Panthenol
(Provitamin B5)
1 vitamin A capsule
6 drops walnut oil

This soothing, smoothing gel contains top-quality active ingredients to moisturize the eye area. It is just right for use in the skin-drying winter months.

■ Dissolve the gelling agent in the distilled water (to thicken the aqueous stage), then add the D-Panthenol in drops. Break open the vitamin A capsule and add the contents to the mixture.

■ To finish, add the walnut oil in drops and stir until the mixture is smooth.

■ Transfer the eye gel to a small, clean jar and wrap decoratively. Apply to smooth minor eye wrinkles. The gel will keep in a very cool place for 3–4 weeks.

MATERIALS

Small, clean jar with
lid

Lip Balm

INGREDIENTS

⅓ oz/10 g un-
bleached beeswax
pastilles (pellets)
1 vitamin E capsule
1 tsp honey
6 drops olive oil
Peppermint essential
oil (optional)

Lip care products make great gifts throughout the year, and especially on Valentine's Day! A hint of mint oil makes this refreshing
balm extra special.

■ Melt the beeswax pellets in a bowl set over a pan of simmering water and let cool slightly before adding the contents of the
vitamin E capsule and the other ingredients, stirring to combine.

■ Transfer the lip balm to a small, clean jar with a sealable lid.
You can add a drop of refreshing mint oil at this stage, if you wish.

GIFT
INSPIRATION

Presented in a pretty
but simple box, this
is a personal gift that
your friends are sure to
appreciate.

MATERIALS

Small, clean jar
with a lid

Festive Orange Wreath

MATERIALS

14 dried orange slices
Wicker wreath (to fit door width)
Florist's wire
5 cinnamon sticks
Ribbon
Pliers

Add a seasonal touch to your friends' homes (and your own) with this fragrant door wreath made of dried orange slices. It would make a thoughtful gift with a difference for friends in the Advent and holiday season.

▦ Attach the orange slices to the wicker wreath using florist's wire, overlapping the slices slightly as shown in the illustration. Leave a clear section about 2¾ inches/7 cm wide at the top for the cinnamon sticks.

▦ Make a small bundle of the cinnamon sticks and attach them to the wreath with florist's wire. Thread the ribbon through the wreath so that it can be hung on a door. Finish by tying a pretty bow around the cinnamon sticks.

Scented Orange Pomander

MATERIALS

Oranges, unwaxed if available
Whole cloves
8 tbsp ground cinnamon
2 tbsp ground orris root powder
1 tbsp grated nutmeg
1 tbsp ground allspice
4 tbsp ground cloves

Pomanders are very simple to make and will add a lasting spicy scent to a room. Enjoy these aromatic oranges, studded with cloves, throughout Advent, and beyond.

▦ Insert the whole cloves in the skin of the oranges in a decorative pattern.

▦ Mix the spices in a bowl and roll the oranges studded with the whole cloves in the mixture until thoroughly coated.

TIP

The oranges will slowly dry out and make a wonderfully fragrant holiday present.

Gentle Furniture Polish

2 unwaxed lemons
Vinegar
Water
2 drops olive oil

Materials

Small cotton cloths
Glass jars

This gentle furniture polish is environmentally friendly and makes a perfect and practical present for those who dislike standard cleaning materials. The soaked cotton cloths also look very pretty in their jars.

■ Mix the vinegar with twice the volume of water, add the olive oil. Store the polish in glass jars. Remove the peel from the lemons in thin strips with a peeler.

■ Soak the cloths in the polish, wring out, and store in separate glass jars, together with the lemon peel.

Tip

Wash the cloths out and resoak. They keep on going!

Wood
Cleaner

INGREDIENTS

1 cup/250 ml
malt vinegar
1 cup/250 ml
turpentine
1 cup/250 ml pure
natural linseed oil
1 tbsp sugar

MATERIALS

Small bottle with
tightly sealed lid

This gift provides the ideal solution for those who love old wooden furniture but don't like the residue that ordinary wood polishes leave behind. It reaches those parts that other cleaners are unable to!

■ Place all the ingredients in a bottle with a tightly sealed lid and shake gently to mix.

■ This wood cleaner can be used on furniture to remove the deposits of old polish that make wood look gray and unattractive. Simply apply with a cloth and buff. The mixture will clean and care for the wood.

TIP

Make sure the bottle is labeled not for internal consumption and keep away from children.

Mother's Day

Mother's Day marks a very special celebration. The tradition harks back to the British and American women's rights movements of the early 20th century. In this busy, time-poor, technological world, we should celebrate unstinting, self-sacrificing maternal love, although plenty of mothers would appreciate gifts on other days of the year, too!

For the Home and Garden

The best presents of all are those over which it is clear that a great deal of thought and care has been taken. Flowers from a garden are always a joy to both give and receive, or what about something more unusual, such as a personalised door sign. Those who go to the trouble of making a gift have sacrificed the one thing that is in increasingly short supply nowadays—time. This makes the gift extra special and valued, as does the fact that it is unique and not mass-produced.

Mother's Day Hearts

MATERIALS

Moss heart(s)
Roses

A rose-filled heart is a declaration of love, whether presented on Valentine's or Mother's Day. The message is loud and clear to those lucky enough to receive one.

■ Moss hearts are available in a range of different shapes and sizes. In this project we used a pointed heart with miniature roses and a rounder heart with moss roses. If you can't find ready-made moss hearts, cut a block of floral foam into a heart shape and soak in cold water. Cover with moss, using florist pins to keep it in position and wrap green thread around the moss to further hold it in place.

■ Filled with red roses, a moss heart looks stunning. A little wisp of gyspophila (baby's breath) or a few stems of forsythia will make it extra special.

GIFT
INSPIRATION

A pretty label with a few well-chosen words, or a short poem, would add an extra touch to this thoughtful gift.

Floral Cupcakes

MATERIALS

Floral foam
Sharp knife
Large leaves
Large bead-headed
pins
Paper or silicone
cupcake cases
Pansies, daisies, or
other garden flowers

These charming little flowers are pretending to be cupcakes! They make delightful and attractive gifts, but from the garden rather than the kitchen.

■ Cut 2-inch/5-cm cubes from the floral foam with a sharp knife.

■ Wrap each of the foam cubes in a large leaf and fix with a pin.

■ Place in a cupcake case and top with a single flower. Pansies and daisies work well, but you can add the flower of your choice.

■ To help the flowers last longer, soak the foam in water before cutting into cubes and use silicone, waxed or foil cupcake cases.

TIP

Present the floral cupcakes on a pretty plate or tray.

Lovely Lavender for the Home and Garden

MATERIALS

For the wreath:
Length of thick wire
Sage
Lavender
Additional flowers
Florist's wire
Pliers
Pruning shears
Garden twine

For the sachets:
Dried lavender
flowers
Embroidered bags
or pretty fabric
handkerchiefs
Matching ribbon

Lavender is both beautiful and fragrant. Use it to make a pretty wreath for the garden and scented bags for the home.

▦ To make the wreath, make a loop at one end of the thick wire. Take small amounts of the sage, lavender, and other flowers and, using the florist's wire, attach them to the thick wire until it is covered completely. Trim the stems and close up the wreath by bending the thick wire in a circle and inserting the end through the loop and folding over. Fill in any gaps with more flowers or lavender and finish by attaching a bow made of garden twine.

▦ Small decorative bags filled with dried lavender make the perfect present for scenting a drawer or placing under a pillow to help you get to sleep. The dried flowers can also be wrapped in a pretty handkerchief and tied with a lavender ribbon, of course!

Decorative Plant Labels

GIFT INSPIRATION

Include pots of the relevant herbs identified on the labels as part of the present.

MATERIALS

Wooden stakes, ⅝ inch/1.5 cm in diameter
Drapery (curtain pole) finials
White lacquer or paint
Flowerpots
Hot melt glue
Brush
Pretty ribbons (optional)

This fun idea will bring a smile to the face of any gardening enthusiast. You won't be able to miss these simple but ingenious plant labels. No more herbal mix-ups!

■ Paint the wooden stakes and drapery finials white, then paint the herb names onto the flowerpots.

■ When the paint has dried, assemble the plant labels: hang the flowerpots on the stakes and place the finials on top, fixing them in position with hot melt glue. This works particularly well thanks to its volume and ability to fill the holes in the flowerpots.

■ Let the hot glue cool and tie some pretty ribbon around the finials as a finishing touch, if you like.

Easter Treats

Magical
Beaded Eggs

TIP

If you are short of
time, prestrung
beads are available
in craft stores.

MATERIALS

Seed beads
Beading wire
Plastic eggs
Wood glue
Brush
Flat rhinestones

These colorful eggs decorated with beads make an unusual and eyecatching Easter gift. Stringing the beads takes time, but is definitely worth the effort once you see the finished article.

◼ You will need a generous selection of beads in your chosen color scheme. Thread the beads onto the wire and prepare long rather than shorter lengths of breads to wrap around the egg. In total, you will need approximately 60 inches/1.5 m of beads.

◼ Start at the top of the egg and apply wood glue to a small section at a time. Wrap the string of beads around the egg in circles, making sure the beads are as close as possible to each other. Work your way around the egg down to the base, allowing the glue to dry a little at each stage in order not to dislodge the beads already in position.

◼ Decorate each end of the egg with a rhinestone in a matching or contrasting color.

Wooden Ducks

MATERIALS

Wooden board,
approx. ½ in/1 cm
thick
Coping saw (fretsaw)
Sandpaper, 100 grit
Small auger
Wooden skewers
Wood glue
Yellow paint (and
orange/brown,
optional)
Brush

These cute wooden ducks are very happy in their flowery meadow, but they will be just as at home on a dining table at Easter or on a shelf in the playroom.

▦ Trace the duck templates (see page 166) onto the wooden board. Cut out the bodies and feet with a coping saw and smooth the edges with sandpaper.

▦ Make a small hole in the base of each duck and in the center of each "foot" with a drill bit or small auger. Mount each duck on a base using the wooden skewer and fix with wood glue.

▦ When the glue has dried, paint the ducks yellow. If you want to add more detail, give them orange beaks, brown legs and feet, and paint in eyes on either side of the head.

Easter Mug

MATERIALS

White mug
China marker
(chinagraph pencil)
Fine brush
Ceramic paints in
black, red, green,
yellow, pink, and
light blue

This little blue hare is hiding in the garden or backyard, ready to embark on an exciting Easter egg hunt.

■ Use a china marker to draw an outline of the hare and flowers on the mug. Fill in the shapes with paint and let dry. Rub off the china marker lines and paint in the details: colorful flower centers and pink ears.

■ Paint the outlines of the hare, flowers, and further detail in black with care (it will be difficult to remove any mistakes).

■ Fire the cup in the oven as instructed on the paint packaging (approx. 30 minutes at 340°F/170°C).

NB If you try out your design in advance on a paper template, make sure it is removed before firing.

Nature's Frozen Garden

VARIATION

Use other shapes to make different ice sculptures, such as stars.

MATERIALS

2 bowls of different sizes
Sprigs of winter foliage and berries
Stones to keep the small bowl in place
Tea lights or pillar candles, as required

These delicate ice bowls look stunning, although they don't last forever. Use berries and leaves suspended in ice to decorate your balcony or garden in fall and winter.

▓ The two bowls must be of different sizes in order to create an ice wall between them at least 1¼ inches/3 cm thick.

▓ Arrange sprigs of winter foliage, such as holly and pine, and berries in the largest bowl, including around the sides. Place the smaller bowl inside the larger one and fill the gap between the two with water. Weigh the smaller bowl down with stones to prevent it from floating up.

▓ Place the bowls in the freezer. Once the water has frozen, remove the bowls and you will have a fabulous transparent container that can even be used as a lantern or candleholder.

Driftwood Guardian Angel

MATERIALS

Old scrap of wood, tapered at the base
Pencil
Sticky tape
Emulsion paint in white and pale pink
Brush
Marker pen in brown
Coconut fibers
Florist's wire
Old piece of tin for the wings
Glue
Tinsnips
Scissors

An angel to watch over you and bring you glad tidings of joy and peace makes a thoughtful gift, and this one is made from recycled material, too! Perfect.

■ Sketch the outline of an angel on the piece of wood with a pencil. Cut out a heart shape from the sticky tape, and place the heart in the middle of the angel's robes. When you paint the angel, this will leave a heart-shaped space.

■ Paint the angel's robes white and the face pale pink. Let dry, draw in the face with marker pen, and attach the coconut fiber as hair using florist's wire. Remove the sticky tape heart. Glue the wings to the back of the piece of wood.

■ If you are unable to find suitable metal wings, carefully cut a pair out of tin using tinsnips (beware sharp edges). Wings made with florist's wire also look good.

Rustic Bark Star

Ruler, pencil,
and paper
Tree bark
Box cutter (utility
knife)
Hot melt glue
Packing string
Small tacks

This decorative and original star made from strips of tree bark is simple and homely.

■ Using a ruler and pencil, draw a star shape, no larger than 8½ inches/22 cm in width, on a sheet of paper and cut it out.

■ Cut the bark into 2¾-inch/7-cm wide strips and arrange them lengthwise in layers, using the star shape as a template. Glue the overlapping strips of bark together with hot melt glue and fix in place with packing string. Build up further layers around the star shape, continuing to glue and tie them, until you have reached the required size.

■ Once the glue holding the star in place has hardened, remove the packing string and nail the strips of bark together with small tacks from the inner and outer edges

■ Insert a length of packing string through the top to use as a loop to hang the star and tie off.

TIP

If you are unable to find any felled trees from which to peel the bark, it should be available at your local florist.

Birch Bark Lantern

Birch bark
Straight-sided jar
Marker pen
Star-shaped
template
Box cutter (utility
knife)
Glue
Packing string
(optional)
Red candle

This attractive winter decoration is made from birch bark and makes a great gift for nature lovers.

■ Cut the birch bark to the dimensions of the jar (to cover the sides of the jar only, not the base). Using the marker pen, draw several star shapes onto the birch bark, then cut them out carefully with the box cutter.

■ Gently bend the bark around the jar. It should bend easily as the bark should have retained the curvature of the tree trunk.

■ To finish, glue the bark to the jar and hold in place with packing string if necessary. Place a red candle in the jar and it will give off a warm light.

Gorgeous Gold Cards

Construction paper
in a light rust color
Folded card in a dark
rust color
Brush
Gilding size
Gold leaf
Stippling brush
Tracing paper
Gold calligraphy pen
Glue
Scissors

These glittering gilt Christmas cards are individual and stylish. As small works of art, they will be the stars of the festive show.

▓ Cut the construction paper to size; it should be a little smaller than the front of the folded card. Use a brush to paint the construction paper with gilding size, leaving a clear border of card around all 4 edges. Let dry, usually to a "tack," according to the manufacturer's instructions.

▓ Apply the gold leaf, carefully pressing it on with the stippling brush. Remove any excess gold and let dry.

▓ Using the gold calligraphy pen, write your message across the tracing paper in a decorative font. Cut to size as required, place in the center of the gilded construction paper, and glue in position. Finally, glue the construction paper assembly to the front of the folded card.

Twinkling Star Cards

MATERIALS

Gift cards made from handmade paper
Pencil
Gilding size
Gold leaf
Stippling brush
Glue
Red cording
Small red tassle
Thin gold giftwrapping ribbon

Twinkle, twinkle little star! These stars make festive decorations for any holiday season card, and the edging adds a pretty and personal touch.

▧ Use a pencil to draw a star on the front of the handmade paper card. Coat the star with gilding size and let dry, usually to a "tack," according to the manufacturer's instructions. Apply the gold leaf, pressing down carefully with the stippling brush and removing the excess.

▧ You can also make a negative image of the star shape, gilding around the star, as the card on the left (above). Once dry, glue on the cording in a wave shape around the edges of the card.

▧ To finish, attach a small tassle, or, so that the card can be hung from a display such as a card garland, add a small loop made from giftwrapping ribbon.

Beaded Wire Baskets

MATERIALS

Florist's wire
Crystal beads and stars
Pliers
Small bowl or jar to use as a template

These charming baskets are made from florist's wire and a few beads. Add a simple bauble and you have a stylish Christmas gift to take to your friends or hosts.

■ Thread the beads and stars onto the florist's wire at intervals. Wind and wrap the decorated wire around a small jar or bowl to create a basket shape.

■ The basket should be fairly rigid, so twist the wire at intervals to give it extra stability and flatten the base so it won't wobble.

■ For a larger basket, just use a larger bowl as a template.

Stylish Popsicle Stick Basket

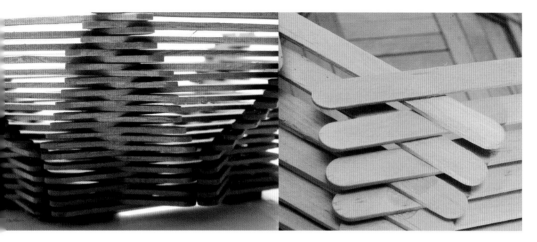

TIP

Keep the distances between the sticks as even as possible, to creat the best visual effect.

MATERIALS

Popsicle sticks in large quantities (available at craft stores)
Woodstain in color of your choice
Rubber household gloves
Wood glue
Rack (e.g. an old oven rack) for drying the basket

It helps to be fond of popsicles if you are planning to make these fun baskets because you are going to need lots and lots of them! Your reward is a beautiful geometric bowl.

▨ Using gloves, dip the popsicle sticks in the colored woodstain and let dry on a rack.

▨ Start with the base. Line up 12 sticks side by side to form a square, then glue 2 sticks at right angles at opposite sides of the square to hold the base together. Let dry.

▨ To make a pentagon shape, glue 4 sticks across the corners of the square, then glue a second row of 4 more sticks diagonally across the corners of those (this row will be in line with the basket bottom), then another 4 (in line with the first row), and carry on building up the sides; each row crosses the corner below it diagonally.

▨ The basket looks best if you bow out the sides slightly. Or taper the sides toward the center at the top, leaving you with an individual designer piece you can give as a gift.

Perfect Paper Gift Box

TIP

You can also place your gift inside the box on a bed of straw or some other filling, but leave it half open when presenting it.

MATERIALS

Wallpaper paste
Waste paper (old printed paper, newspaper, etc.)
Brush

Telephone directories, old printed documents, and yesterday's newspapers can be transformed into useful recycled gift boxes from preloved paper.

◼ Mix the wallpaper paste according to the directions on the packet. This is applied to the strips of paper where they overlap. Fold the sheets of paper into strips ½–¾ inches/1.5–2 cm wide— each strip should be several layers thick.

◼ Starting at the bottom, start to coil the strips of paper, placing each one slightly above the previous one, in order to form a round bowl shape, glueing in place with the wallpaper paste as you go. This should allow you to hide the joins between each strip of paper.

◼ Repeat so that you have two bowl shapes and let dry. Use a final strip of paper around one of the bowls in order to make a lid. Place the two bowls together to form a spherical gift box.

Newspaper Basket

MATERIALS

Newspapers
1 long, thin knitting needle
Sticky tape

Newspapers are ephemeral. Yesterday's headlines are old news (literally!), and newspapers are really only good for recycling. Try transforming them into pretty gift baskets instead.

▧ Roll up the individual pages of the newspaper as tightly as possible around a knitting needle. Prepare a good number of these paper rolls in advance, holding them together with a small piece of sticky tape.

▧ Place 14 newspaper strips one on top of the other to form a multi-pointed star shape. Secure in the center with a small piece of sticky tape. These will form the frame through which the other strips are woven, as if you were weaving a basket.

▧ Weave strips in and out of this frame in a spiral to form a flat base, making sure the strips of the multi-pointed star shape are spread out at more or less equal intervals. You can join a new strip of paper to the end of the previous one with a small piece of sticky tape.

▧ Once the base is the size you require, bend the frame strips upward and continue weaving the basket in and out of them until the sides reach a height of 4 inches/10 cm. The basket is now complete and any remaining frame strips sticking out can be tucked back inside the basket.

▧ Using shorter paper strips, make the lid in the same way as the base; it should be slightly wider than the top of the basket. To finish, make 2 handles from twisted strips of paper and pull them through the center of the lid, fixing them on the inside with sticky tape.

SIZE OF FINISHED BASKET

Diameter:
14 inches/35 cm
Height: 4 inches/
10 cm

Welcome Sign

GIFT INSPIRATION

Write a welcome message on the board and hang it where your friends will see it.

MATERIALS

Self-adhesive film
Craft knife
Wooden board, cut to the appropriate size
Blackboard paint
Stippling brush
Small nails
Colored packing string or cord, as required
Hook
Sponge
Chalk
Fabric hearts
Glue

This wooden door sign makes a lovely present for friends who have just moved house or for new arrivals in the neighborhood.

▥ Trace the bird template (see page 166) onto the self-adhesive film and carefully cut out with the craft knife.

▥ Stick the film to the wooden board and press down firmly. Apply the blackboard paint to the board with the stippling brush; the template will act like a stencil and protect the bare wood underneath. Let dry and remove the film to reveal the bird shape and border.

▥ Knock two small nails into the sides or front of the board and tie on a length of packing string or cord.

▥ A large board can be used for shopping or To Do lists. Use the alternative template and make the blackboard area as large as you like. Attach a hook to one side and tie an eraser (a sponge cut to size with scissors) and chalk to it. Small hearts cut out of fabric can be used as additional decorations.

Wrapped
with Love

Gifts show your appreciation of others, while how you wrap them can also express your affection. However, that doesn't mean that paper has to be folded immaculately or a bow attached with great precision. Individuality and originality are much more important. Small wooden boxes, sisal bags, or even newspaper work well. Homemade wrapping is a gift in itself and won't simply be thrown away once the gift has been unwrapped. Sustainability and recycling also play a key role. You won't need to make a trip to the store for most of these wrapping ideas—you'll find all the materials in your own home. It's time to really enjoy wrapping and packing!

Stylish Stamps and Pretty String

TIP

These stamps will also brighten up your holiday notepaper and envelopes.

MATERIALS

Pencil
4–5 large erasers (or rubber carving blocks)
Linoleum knife
Packing paper (cream, white, beige, natural)
Blue and red printing ink
Red-and-white string

Plain packing paper, a few homemade rubber stamps, a splash of printing ink, and some red-and-white string: these are the ingredients for perfect personalized wrapping paper.

■ Using a pencil, trace your design (for example, the stag or pine tree from the template on page 167) onto an eraser or rubber block. Create a stamp by cutting out the design with a linoleum knife and carefully removing the surrounding rubber to a depth of about $1/16$ inch/2 mm.

■ Press the rubber stamp into the printing ink and print the design onto the packing paper in rows, at angles, upside down, or at random—however you wish—and let dry.

■ All you need to complete the wrapping and make a perfect package is a length of red-and-white string.

Woven Gift Ribbons

Add a rustic twist with some woven raffia and jute ribbons.

MATERIALS

Plain cream paper
Ribbons (patterned white, gold, and transparent)
Pins
Glue

Tying neat bows can be the trickiest part of the whole wrapping process. I don't find it easy and sometimes do without one. Here I have woven beautiful gold ribbons around the parcel for a sophisticated look.

▓ Wrap the gift in the plain paper, then weave the ribbons around the parcel in your chosen design, ensuring they overlap slightly at the back.

▓ There is no need to cover the whole package, and you can weave the ribbons in and out in different patterns. It's a good way of using up odds and ends of ribbons, braids, and fabric scraps.

▓ Ensure the ribbons meet at the back of the package and fasten with pins. Once you're satisfied with your woven design, glue the ribbons in place and remove the pins.

Pretty Planters

Wooden planter
Blackboard paint
Brush
Chalk
String (red and white
or other colors)

These wooden planters make ideal containers for canning jars. The sides are painted with practical blackboard paint on which to write a message.

■ Paint one side of the wooden planter with blackboard paint. Let dry and write your message in chalk.

■ Place the jar inside and secure it in place with colored string.

■ As an alternative, instead of blackboard paint use small labels cut out of wrapping paper or small wooden signs.

Hide 'n' Peek

MATERIALS

Sisal bags
Wooden clothespins
(pegs)
Ribbon or cord
Small, thin scraps of
wooden board for
gift tags
Small pieces of
driftwood
Scissors

These simple sisal bags both contain and reveal the contents at the same time—in this case, jars of tasty jams and preserves.

■ Close the bags with a traditional wooden clothespin or tie with a pretty ribbon or cord.

■ Carefully pierce a hole in the end of a small piece of wooden board with the point of the scissors and thread through a length of cord or ribbon as a gift tag. Decorate the bag by tying on a small piece of driftwood, collected on your last beach vacation.

TIP

You can buy
old-style wooden
clothespins from
stores or online.

It's a Wrap!

Textured paper
Glue
Hole punch
Wooden sticks
Stickers
Calligraphy pen
Scissors

These pretty bags are quick to make and are ideal for wrapping spices, tea, and herbs.

▨ Using the template (page 167), cut out the bag from the textured paper and fold it as indicated; the top part forms a flap. Glue the two sides together along the tab (see template). Using the hole punch, make corresponding holes in opposite sides of the bag and the flap for the wooden stick.

▨ Write your message on a sticker with the calligraphy pen and attach to the bag, then fill it with your chosen gift. Insert the stick through the punched holes to close the bag.

▨ Wallpaper swatches or gift wrap are good substitutes for textured paper, while bags made from comic books or magazines will certainly raise a smile!

TIP

Place the tea, herbs, or spices in small cellophane bags first, so that they don't spill out.

It's in the Bag!

MATERIALS

Paper bags
Silver or gold paper
embossed edging
Glue
Scissors

These embossed borders bring more than a hint and a glint of glamor to simple paper bags that are very eco-friendly.

■ Trim the bags so they are almost square in size before attaching the edging strip to the top edge with glue. Place your gift inside the bag.

■ Scrapbook pictures often have beautiful borders and can also be used to decorate the bags. Sections of paper doily can be used to make pretty borders, too.

TIP

Match the color of the bag with the border if possible.

Favorite Things
Tied up with String

TIP

Packing string, sisal, and raffia make stylish gift ties.

MATERIALS

Cardboard tubes
Wrapping paper
(with or without
handwritten text)
Packing string
Gift tags (or old
greetings cards cut
up and recycled as
tags)
Hole punch
Scissors

A whole host of surprises can be concealed in these party cracker-inspired packages: candies, scarves, or even an engagement ring could be secreted inside! And if you want to make a very special effort for the object of your affection, write a poem, story, or declaration of love on the wrapping paper itself.

▥ Place your gift in a cardboard tube and wrap in the paper (with or without a special message). Trim the ends to the desired length and twist together or tuck neatly inside the tube (providing the contents won't fall out). Tie the packing string around the center, leaving enough string to thread through a gift tag.

▥ Write your message on a gift tag, punch a hole through one end and attach it to the packing string.

Decorate with Felt

VARIATION

You can make a variety of shapes if you have a selection of cookie cutters.

MATERIALS

Cookie cutters
Vanishing fabric marker
Felt fabric (1/16 inch/ 2 mm thick) in gray and red
Fabric cutter
Sewing machine or sewing needle
Sewing thread in gray
Hole punch
Leather laces in white
Scissors

These pretty felt stars will brighten up any gift or can be used as decorations in their own right. The decorations shown opposite are machine-sewn, but look just as lovely when made entirely by hand.

▥ Using a cookie cutter as a template, draw the design on the felt with the vanishing fabric marker. You can use a fabric cutter to cut around the edge of the cookie cutter or cut out the design with scissors.

▥ Quilt around the edges of the felt decorations and quilt a design of your choice in the center, such as a heart or flower.

▥ Make a hole in the top of each decoration with the hole punch, thread through a leather lace, stand back, and admire!

Signed, Sealed, and Delivered

VARIATION

A gift tag made of textured paper rolled up like a scroll and also fixed with a seal will add the finishing touch.

MATERIALS

Tissue paper in light gray
Double-sided sticky tape
Leather laces in red
Silk ribbon in red
Wrapping ribbon in red
Metallic string in red
Sealing wax in red
Seal
Scissors

Tying the perfect knot can be a challenge, making sealing wax the ideal alternative. The leather laces, metallic string, and ribbons are wrapped around the gift several times and fixed in place with the wax.

▧ Wrap your gift in tissue paper, sealing with double-sided sticky tape (rather than ordinary, more visible tape).

▧ Use leather laces, ribbons, or string to bind the package and seal the ends together with sealing wax. To do this, heat the sealing wax with a candle, let it drip where required, and press the seal into the wax before it hardens.

▧ Alternatively, add sealing wax to ends of the ribbon or in the center of the package, where the ribbon, string, or laces cross.

Natural Expression

Wooden Boxes
with Raffia Ties

VARIATION

As a natural material, raffia is also a good choice for wrapping up foodstuffs like these vanilla beans.

MATERIALS

Plain wooden boxes
Raffia
Softwood shavings
Handmade paper
Calligraphy pen
(optional)
Glue
Quail eggs, blown
White feathers
Scissors

These simple wooden boxes are reminiscent of the understated charm of Shaker boxes. Add a little raffia, some quail eggs, and a few feathers to make a special package.

▓ Fill the box with raffia or softwood shavings and place your gift inside it.

▓ Cut out a piece of handmade paper slightly smaller than the box and write a personal message on it—use a calligraphy pen if you wish (poems, thoughts, and good wishes are always appreciated when written neatly by hand). Place the paper inside the box, or write a message on a smaller piece of paper and glue it to the top of the box.

▓ Bind the box with raffia, wrapping it around once or twice. Thread one of the ends through the hole in the quail egg and decorate with a feather.

Bag Full of News

This unusual bag uses recycled materials and when you've finished with it, can be recycled itself. It is surprisingly strong, too!

▦ Choose a book of the required size and shape to use as a template for the bag. Place the book on two sheets of the paper (one on top of the other) and cut the paper to the required width—it should be slightly wider than the longer side of the book. Make sure an attractive section of the newspaper will be on show at the front of the bag (adverts, photos, attractive fonts, etc.).

▦ Place the book on the paper about two thirds down, with the spine facing you. Fold up the edge nearest you over the book and tuck it under the front cover to form a small flap. Remove the book and glue the flap down. Replace the book. The third of the paper above the book will form the bag's front flap. If you find that the paper isn't long enough, simply add an extra section. Snip into this on either side of the book so that you can fold in the two edges to create a front flap that fits the bag. Glue the edges down. Fold down the top of the front flap to hide the glued edges, and glue down. Fold in the sides of the bag over the book as you would when wrapping a present and glue them down.

▦ Glue together strips of newspaper long enough to make a strap; it will go around the whole bag to give it rigidity. Fold it lengthways to make a strap the width of the bag—it should be several layers of paper thick. Glue the strap in place, fixing it on three sides of the bag. Let the glue dry. Remove the book, and your eco-friendly paper bag is ready.

MATERIALS

Newspaper pages (foreign-language papers add a nice touch)
Book, to use as a template
Glue
Scissors

GIFT INSPIRATION

A gift label made from wrapping paper with a hole punched through and threaded onto packing string adds a nice touch and is in keeping with the style of the gift itself.

Papier-mâché Pebbles

These pebble boxes have a simple elegance and a practical application. They are easy to make, and may conceal treasure!

▓ Tear the tissue paper into 1-inch/2.5-cm squares. Make up the wallpaper paste according to the directions and let expand.

▓ Coat a part of the stone with wallpaper paste and layer the pieces of tissue paper on top, brushing with more paste as you apply each piece.

▓ Once you have completely covered the top of the stone with enough layers of tissue paper, place it upside down on an eggcup or jar and complete the other side.

▓ Once the papier-mâché has dried completely, use a sharp knife to cut off the top and remove the stone.

▓ To make the cut-off top into a lid, place it on the stone and add some more papier-mâché around the edge to enlarge it so that it overlaps the base slightly. Let the lid dry, trim the edges, and attach it to the base with a hinge made from a few pieces of tissue paper. Now you can fill the pebble gift box with the gift of your choice.

▓ Stamp a design on a luggage label and attach it to the pebble box with some sisal string or raffia. This pretty gift box can be used again and again.

MATERIALS

For the pebble boxes:
Tissue paper in gray
Wallpaper paste
Brush
Large stone
Eggcup or jar
Sharp knife
Scissors

For the labels:
Luggage labels
Stamp with design of your choice
Stamping ink in metallic copper
Sisal string or raffia

TIP

Use large stones about 2¾–4 inches/ 7–10 cm in diameter.

Index

Blanket stitch

duck base

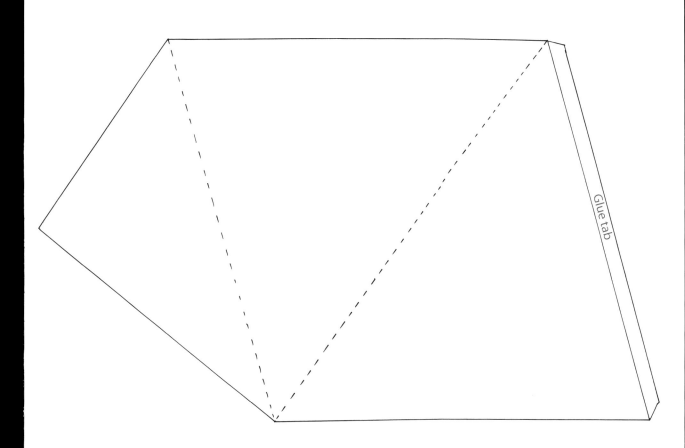

Glue tab

Abbreviations and quantities
1 oz = 1 ounce = 28 grams
1 lb = 1 pound = 16 ounces
1 cup = 8 ounces = 16 ounces
1 cup = 8 fluid ounces = 250 milliliters
(liquids)
2 cups = 1 pint (liquids)
8 pints = 4 quarts = 1 gallon (liquids)
1g = 1 gram = 1/1000 kilogram
1kg = 1 kilogram = 1000 grams = 2 ¼ lb
1 l = 1 liter = 1000 milliliters (ml) = approx
34 fluid ounces
125 milliliters (ml) = approx. 8 tablespoons
1 tbsp = 1 level tablespoon = 15–20g (see
below) = 15 milliliters (liquids)
1 tsp = 1 level teaspoon = 3–5g (see
below) = 5ml (liquids)

Where measurements of dry ingredients
are given in spoons, this always refers to
the prepared ingredient as described in
the wording immediately following, e.g.
1 tbsp chopped onions BUT: 1 onion,
peeled and chopped.